CONTENTS

INTRODUCING NATIONAL 5 MODERN STUDIES

Political issues, like who has the power in a country or the decisions governments make, and social issues, like inequality and crime, exist in Scotland and all around the world. In the 21st century, the world we live in has never been more closely connected. Through the internet, 24-hour news channels and social media we are bombarded with information and opinion on all sort of issues.

Modern Studies aims to use the social sciences of politics, sociology, economics and others to help students make sense of these issues, and form well-thought-out and balanced opinions about them.

Knowing about these topics is not going to be enough when it comes to being successful in your future career; you also need to be able to communicate with others about what you know, sharing your information and opinion in a number of ways. National 5 aims to equip you with these skills as well as knowledge.

THE BENEFITS OF NATIONAL 5

National 5 Modern Studies is a course that allows you to develop an in-depth understanding of many of the most important and interesting issues in Scottish and/ or UK politics, UK society and in or between important countries or international organisations.

The course will equip you with a range of skills to help you be a confident individual and effective contributor in your further studies, your chosen career and your wider life. These include the skills of effective research, understanding and analysing a range of competing information, working with other people, and communicating/presenting what you know and understand.

THE EXTERNAL ASSESSMENT: COMPONENT 1 – QUESTION PAPER

The Course Assessment will be what decides your grade for National 5 Modern Studies. This course can be passed with a grade from the highest (A) down to a C. The Question Paper is worth 60 marks (75% of the total marks). Most of these marks are for knowledge and understanding, and the rest are for source-based skills questions.

You will have 1 hour and 30 minutes to complete the Question Paper.

The Question Paper will measure the breadth and application of your learning, and challenge you to show how much you understand the course.

Breadth, application and challenge

The Course Assessment will test your knowledge and understanding from three units (each worth 20 marks):
- Democracy in Scotland and the United Kingdom
- Social Issues in the United Kingdom
- International Issues

Knowledge and understanding

In each unit, you are expected to be able to give detailed descriptions and explanations, using factual and theoretical knowledge of each unit.

This means that not only do you have to know facts and figures about these

contd

ED Study Guide

riculum for Excellence

N5

MODERN STUDIES

Kirsty Marsland, Caleb Marwick and Heidi Stoutjesdyk

First published in 2013 by:
Bright Red Publishing Ltd
1 Torphichen Street
Edinburgh
EH3 8HX

A CIP record for this book is available from the British Library.

ISBN 978-1-906736-42-2

With thanks to:
PDQ Digital Media Solutions Ltd, Bungay (layout), Anglosphere Editing Ltd (editorial). Cover design and series book design by Caleb Rutherford – eidetic.

Acknowledgements
Every effort has been made to seek all copyright-holders. If any have been overlooked, then Bright Red Publishing will be delighted to make the necessary arrangements.

Permission has been sought from all relevant copyright holders and Bright Red Publishing is grateful for the use of the following:

Saül Gordillo (p 7); Logos © The Conservative Party, The Labour Party, The Liberal Democrats & The Scottish National Party (p 8); Ian Murray (p 9); Caleb Marwick (p 10); Two Parliamentary copyright images reproduced with the permission of Parliament (p 12); Duirinish Light/Shutterstock.com (p 18); Two images © Scottish Parliamentary Corporate Body – 2012. Licensed under the Open Scottish Parliament Licence v1.0. (pp 19 & 20); Lance Bellers/Shutterstock.com (p 24); Sagaciousphil/Creative Commons (CC BY-SA 3.0)[1] (p 25); Malcolm Bell (p 26); Nick Cook (p 26); City of Edinburgh Council (p 26); Carrie Ann Images/Creative Commons (CC BY-ND 2.0)[2] (p 27); Malcolm Bell (p 27); Liberal Democrats/Creative Commons (CC BY-ND 2.0)[2] (p 28); Scots Independent Collection, Scottish Political Archive, University of Stirling www.scottishpoliticalarchive.org.uk (p 29); An image from http://www.scotland.gov.uk/Resource/Doc/345798/0115097.pdf © Crown Copyright 2011 (p 34); Logos © The Conservative Party, The Scottish National Party, The Labour Party, The Scottish Green Party, The Liberal Democrats & Scottish Socialist Party (p 34); Logos © National Farmers Union (Scotland), British Medical Association (Scotland), Greenpeace, Animal Liberation Front (public domain), Pedal on Parliament, The TaxPayers' Alliance & The Robin Hood Tax (p 36); Logos © UK Uncut & Greenpeace (p 37); Logos © Equity, Aslef & Unite (p 38); Logo © TUC/Image © Ljupco Smokovski/Shutterstock.com (p 38); landmarkmedia/Shutterstock.com (p 40); Photos of Gordon Brown and David Cameron licensed under the Open Government Licence v2.0. (p 41); World Economic Forum swiss-image.ch/Photo by Moritz Hager/Creative Commons (CC BY-SA 2.0)[3] (p 41); Andrew Milligan/PA Archive/Press Association Images (p 41); A headline from BBC News online 25 April 2013 © BBC News (p 42); A headline from The Scotsman online, 22 April 2013 © 2013 Johnston Publishing Ltd. (p 43); A headline from The Herald 21 April 2013 © Herald & Times Group (p 43); Logos © Twitter, Inc., Facebook, YouTube, LLC & Mumsnet Limited (p 43); Kovnir Andrii/Shutterstock.com (p 48); 1000 Words/Shutterstock.com (p 50); Monkey Business Images/Shutterstock.com (p 52); An extract from the article 'Men in Glasgow's east end have life expectancy of 54', by Lachlan MacKinnon, takne from the Daily Record 29th August 2008 © Mirrorpix (p 58); John Fleming/Creative Commons (CC BY-SA 3.0)[1] (p 58); shirokazan/Creative Commons (CC BY 2.0)[4] (p 58); BaLL LunLa/Shutterstock.com (p 59); bikeriderlondon/Shutterstock.com (p 61); Andy Dean Photography/Shutterstock.com (p 64); Mega Pixel/Shutterstock.com (p 66); Domofon/Shutterstock.com (p 67); Graeme Maclean/Creative Commons (CC BY 2.0)[4] (p 68); I See Modern Britain/Creative Commons (CC BY 2.0)[4] (p 73); RonAlmog/Creative Commons (CC BY 2.0)[4] (p 76); Chris Upson/Creative Commons (CC BY-SA 2.0)[3] (p 78); Polmont Young Offenders Institution photo licensed under the Open Government Licence v2.0. (p 81); Flag of Brazil (public domain) (p 86); Agência Brasil/Creative Commons (CC BY 3.0 BR)[5] (p 89); Neil Palmer/CIAT/Creative Commons (CC BY-SA 2.0)[3] (p 90); Flag of India (public domain) (p 92); dp Photography/Shutterstock.com (p 94); OlegD/Shutterstock.com (p 96); Agência Brasil/Creative Commons (CC BY 3.0 BR)[5] (p 97); Logos © The National Rifle Association of America & National Right to Life (p 99); Rakkhi Samarasekera/Creative Commons (CC BY 2.0)[4] (p 100); U.S. Navy photo by Mass Communication Specialist 2nd Class Jesse B. Awalt (public domain) (p 104); Logo © United Nations (p 104); Logos © UNICEF, WHO, UNHCR, World Food Programme & United Nations Development Programme (p 105); Logo © Amnesty International (p 106); Petty Officer 2nd Class Ernesto Hernandez Fonte/DVIDSHUB/Creative Commons (CC BY 2.0)[4] (p 108); Grüne Bundestagsfraktion/Creative Commons (CC BY 2.0) (p 109); U.S. Signal Corps (public domain) (p 113); Logo © Child Soldiers International (p 114); UNDP Brazil (p 116); Philip Date/Shutterstock.com (p 119); © UNICEF/ETHA2013_00488/Ose (p 123).

[1](CC BY-SA 3.0) http://creativecommons.org/licenses/by-sa/3.0/
[2] (CC BY-ND 2.0) http://creativecommons.org/licenses/by-nd/2.0/
[3](CC BY-SA 2.0) http://creativecommons.org/licenses/by-sa/2.0/
[4](CC BY 2.0) http://creativecommons.org/licenses/by/2.0/
[5](CC BY 3.0 BR) http://creativecommons.org/licenses/by/3.0/br/deed.en

Printed and bound in the UK by Martins the Printers.

issues, but you also need to know about possible reasons for, and points of view about, each topic or issue.

Skills questions

In these questions you will be given between two and four sources of information, containing a mixture of words and numbers, and be able to:

- detect and explain, in detail, exaggeration or selective use of facts (pages 44–47)
- make and justify, in detail, a decision, and discuss the opposite choice and points of view (pages 80–81)
- draw and support, in detail, a conclusion (pages 120–121).

For each of these types of question, you will need to give detailed descriptions and explanations, with some analysis.

THE EXTERNAL ASSESSMENT: COMPONENT 2 – ASSIGNMENT

The Assignment is worth 20 marks (25% of the total mark).

Unlike the Question Paper, the Assignment has more marks available for skills than knowledge and understanding.

You will have up to 1 hour to complete the Assignment.

The Assignment will ask you to: choose an appropriate Modern Studies topic or issue; collect evidence on this topic from at least two different types of source/research methods; discuss the strengths and weaknesses of these research methods, and how useful they are; apply your source-based skills to the collected evidence; explain and analyse the topic studied, using your Modern Studies knowledge and understanding; and reach a well-supported conclusion, with evidence, about the topic.

THE MANDATORY UNITS

As well as the final Course Assessment, you must pass all three units:

- Democracy in Scotland and the United Kingdom
- Social Issues in the United Kingdom
- International Issues

These units will be assessed by your teachers or lecturers, who will be devising their own assessment programmes. Knowing your abilities first-hand, they will decide the most appropriate ways to generate convincing evidence of your performance. Just like the Course Assessment, you will be assessed on knowledge and understanding, and skills questions.

HOW WILL THIS GUIDE HELP YOU MEET THE CHALLENGES?

This guide is designed to give you the best possible chance to succeed in National 5 Modern Studies. Completing the course will not be easy, and you are expected to know a lot, but this book will give you a very strong foundation for achieving a great grade in the course.

Each section contains detailed examples and explanations of the relevant topic, in as user-friendly a way as possible.

Skills questions are approached in the designated spreads.

Throughout this book we promise we will at all times be talking to you and not at you!

Added to the work you complete in school and as homework, use of this book should put you in a really strong position to achieve your potential in National 5 Modern Studies.

ONLINE

This book is supported by the BrightRED Digital Zone - log on at www.brightredbooks.net/N5ModernStudies for a world of tests, activities, videos and more!

THE UK POLITICAL SYSTEM

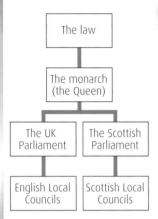

LAYERS OF DECISION MAKING

The UK has layers of decision making. At different levels, different people and organisations make the decisions. Above all, the law in the UK decides what decisions can and cannot be made. Each new law must be officially approved by the monarch (the head of the Royal Family).

The UK Parliament makes decisions that affect the whole of the UK in some areas, known as **reserved matters** (see pages 10–17). The Scottish Parliament, since **devolution**, makes decisions on areas that affect Scotland alone.

Local matters are decided by local councils (see the 'Local councils' and 'Work of local councillors' sections).

FACT

Scottish Devolution Referendum 1997 results
I agree that there should be a Scottish Parliament: 73.4%
I agree that a Scottish Parliament should have tax-varying powers: 63.5%

DEVOLUTION

In 1997, the Labour Party won the UK **general election** and formed the UK Government. They had a **manifesto** promise to hold a **referendum** (a public vote over one decision) on giving Scotland a **parliament** of its own. The referendum passed, and the Scottish Parliament was set up in 1999.

Devolved and reserved matters

Devolved matters	Reserved matters
Agriculture, forestry and fisheries	Benefits and social security
Education and training	Immigration
Environment	Defence
Health and social services	Foreign policy
Housing	Employment
Law and order	Broadcasting
Local government	Trade and industry
Sport and the arts	Nuclear energy, oil, coal, gas and electricity
Tourism and economic development	Consumer rights
Transport	Data protection
	The Constitution

Devolved and reserved matters

The Scottish Parliament was set up to work alongside the UK Parliament in making decisions for Scotland. As such, the power to make laws only in certain areas, which affect only Scotland, was given over to the Scottish Parliament. These **policy** areas are called **devolved matters**, for example education is a devolved matter. This means Scotland can (and unusually has always been able to) create its own education policy. Only students in Scotland study National 5 qualifications, and Modern Studies in fact!

On the other hand, the UK Parliament retains the power to make laws about areas that affect the whole of the UK or have an international impact. These areas are called reserved matters.

THE FUTURE OF SCOTTISH DECISION MAKING

On the 1 May 2012, the UK Parliament passed the Scotland Act (2012). This Act allows the Scottish Parliament to set income tax rates in Scotland and borrow more money: a combined £5 billion in new financial powers. The UK Government described it as the biggest transfer of financial power to Scotland in 300 years.

Other powers, including the regulation of air guns, drink-driving, and speed limits, and a role in broadcasting, and taxes including stamp duty, land tax and landfill tax, will also be devolved. The new powers can only be used from 2016 onwards.

Of course, if Scotland votes 'Yes' to independence in the referendum of 18 September 2014 there will be no more devolved and reserved matters: the Scottish Parliament will

contd

make all the decisions for Scotland. For this reason, the Scottish National Party (SNP) Government has said the Scotland Act 2012 may be 'bypassed by events'.

As the Constitution is a reserved matter, the UK Government had to grant the Scottish Parliament unusual powers in order to hold a referendum, called a Section 30 agreement. The SNP Scottish Government had to negotiate with the UK Government about how and when the referendum would be run. On 15 October 2012, Prime Minister David Cameron and First Minister Alex Salmond signed the agreement on the Scottish referendum deal, which Alex Salmond called the Edinburgh Agreement.

Signing the Edinburgh Agreement

PARLIAMENTS IN THE UK

The UK Parliament has evolved over more than 1000 years, going through many changes in that time. It has evolved to have two houses: the House of Commons and the House of Lords. A parliamentary system with two houses like this is called **bicameral**.

In each chamber, the government and **opposition** (the biggest party that is not in the government) sit on opposite benches, facing each other. This could be seen to encourage confrontation between the parties.

The Scottish Parliament is young in contrast, created new in 1999, with the Scottish Parliament building being completed in 2004. This allowed the Scottish Parliament to take the best parts of the UK system and change the ones that it thought it could do better. There is only one house in the Scottish Parliament, with no equivalent to the House of Lords. A parliamentary system with one house is called **unicameral**.

In the Scottish Parliament chamber the members of the Scottish Parliament (MSPs) sit in a semi-circular arrangement. This could be seen to encourage cooperation between the parties.

Parliament and government

The party (or parties in a **coalition**) that has the most members of parliament (MPs) or MSPs elected forms the **government**. This is the institution which runs the country and introduces the most Bills in the country.

The leader of the winning party in the UK becomes the Prime Minister and is officially asked by the Queen to form the government. In Scotland, however, the First Minister is elected from amongst the MSPs after each Scottish election.

The **Cabinet** is the central group of government members. It coordinates the work of different government departments and decides government policy. The UK Cabinet has about 20 members, while the Scottish Cabinet has around 10 members.

Cabinet meetings happen in private and individual members must support the decisions that the Cabinet makes. This is called **collective responsibility**.

VIDEO LINK

Check out the clip about the House of Commons chamber at www.brightredbooks.net/N5ModernStudies.

VIDEO LINK

Check out the clip about the House of Lords chamber at www.brightredbooks.net/N5ModernStudies.

VIDEO LINK

Watch the video 'The Scottish Parliament' at www.brightredbooks.net/N5ModernStudies.

ONLINE TEST

Test yourself on the UK political system online at www.brightredbooks.net/N5ModernStudies.

THINGS TO DO AND THINK ABOUT

1 Make a spider diagram of devolved and reserved matters.

2 'The Scottish Parliament makes most of the important decisions for Scotland.'

    Do you agree with this statement? Give reasons for your answer.

3 Explain what each of the following terms means in your own words:
   - referendum
   - government
   - Cabinet

4 Find out the name and role of a member of the Scottish or UK Cabinet.

YOUR REPRESENTATIVES

THE NATURE OF REPRESENTATION

Levels of decision making.

Type of issue	Decisions made by	Your representative(s)
Local	Local authority/council	Local councillors (three or four)
Scottish	Scottish Parliament	Constituency MSP Regional MSPs (seven)
National (UK)	UK Parliament	Constituency MP
European	European Parliament	Scotland's MEPs (six)

Each of us is represented by a number of different people, at a number of different levels of decision making. From local councils right up to the European Parliament in Brussels there are people whose job it is to speak up for us and our interests.

DON'T FORGET

At all levels it is the job of representatives to speak on behalf of their constituents.

POLITICAL PARTIES IN THE UK

Most representatives at each level stand for election as members of a political party. Each political party changes its policies in line with circumstances to try and give themselves the best chance to be elected. However, parties do have different **ideologies**: sets of beliefs about how to make Scotland or the UK better. The summaries below are based on the 2010 general election and Scottish election 2011 (SNP) manifestos.

 **Conservatives**

Conservative
- Call on individual citizens to help change the country: the Big Society.
- Encourage parents and organisations in England to set up new academy schools.
- Plan to reverse a proposed National Insurance (a type of tax) rise.
- Have a points system for immigration and a total limit on the number who can enter the UK.
- Raise the inheritance tax threshold (the amount at which you start paying it) to £1m.

 **Labour**

Labour
- Government responsible for changing the country.
- Underperforming schools in England can be taken over by more successful management teams.
- Plan to raise National Insurance.
- Have a points system for immigration, with no limit on the number who can enter the UK.
- Keep the inheritance tax threshold at £325,000 if the deceased was single or £650,000 if the deceased was married or widowed.

Scottish Liberal Democrats

Liberal Democrat
- Government mainly responsible for changing the country.
- In England, a pupil premium of £2.5bn to be given to headteachers to allow average class sizes to be cut to 20 pupils.
- Allow people to earn £10,000 before paying any income tax.
- Have a points system for immigration, but on a regional level, and have no upper limits on who can enter the UK.

 **SNP**

SNP
- Main aim is for Scotland to become independent after a referendum.
- Have the new Curriculum for Excellence as the cornerstone of education in Scotland.
- No tuition fees for Scottish students going to Scottish universities.
- Favour many social benefits for all, like free prescriptions.

There are also a number of minor parties, like the Greens, UKIP (United Kingdom Independence Party) and the BNP, who have different ideologies.

CONTACTING YOUR REPRESENTATIVES

Once elected, an MP or MSP's job is one which involves frequent communication.

contd

From Ian Murray's website

ONLINE

Follow the link at www.brightredbooks.net/N5ModernStudies to find Ian Murray on Twitter.

In order to be able to represent the interests of his/her **constituents** (the people they represent), each representative must be able to hear from them. They provide a number of ways in which to do this. On the official website of the organisation, and their own website, you will be able to find an e-mail address and/or telephone number for the representative. At least from Scottish Parliament level upwards, representatives have **constituency** offices, which you can visit or contact to raise concerns or issues with that representative.

Increasingly, representatives are turning to social media to have instant communication with their constituents. For example, Ian Murray, MP for Edinburgh South, actively uses Twitter (@IanMurrayMP) to get in touch with his constituents and keep them up to date with his work on their behalf.

THE WORK OF MPs AND MSPs IN CONSTITUENCIES

As well as having to be easy to contact by concerned or interested constituents, MPs and MSPs have a great deal of work to do in their constituencies.

MPs and MSPs hold **surgeries** in their constituencies. These are scheduled times when any concerned constituent can come and speak face to face with their representative. Details of when surgeries are to take place will appear on the representative's website and perhaps in the local newspaper. Surgeries allow the representative to hear about the problems or issues their constituents face. The representative can tell the constituent about any work that is already being done on the matter or can take the problem up with the relevant people involved, perhaps in parliament.

MSPs and MPs also often attend social events in their constituencies. This shows an active interest in the people and place they represent. It also allows constituents to informally get to know their representative(s) and see them as more approachable if they do have a problem in the future. Ian Murray MP attended the Buckstone Community Fun Day 2013.

IAN MURRAY MP
Your member of Parliament for
Edinburgh South
Twice Weekly Advice Sessions
Every Monday and friday at 9.15am
At 31 Minto Street
Just drop in – no appointment necessary

Every 3rd Saturday of the month
9am – Gracemount Leisure Centre
10am – Liberton High School
11am – Constituency Office, 31 Minto Street
Noon – The Open Door, 420 Morningside Road

Representatives also go on fact-finding missions to schools, businesses and other organisations in their constituencies. This helps the representative hear about how things are going in their area from the people who are directly involved. This also gives constituents the chance to ask a representative face to face about any issues they're having and what the representative plans to do about it.

On visits to schools, the pupils – constituents who are nearly all too young to vote – get a chance to put really probing questions to their representative. On a visit to Boroughmuir High School in October 2012, Ian Murray MP was asked whether he supported the recent decision to build a new school, rather than renovate the old.

When constituents have raised a concern with their MP or MSP about something that involves a business or other organisation, the MP or MSP may meet with the organisation or organisations involved. By doing this, they hope to find a solution for their constituents that the constituents may not have managed to achieve themselves. Tavish Scott, MSP for Shetland, met with the rail company Scotrail and ferry operator Serco Northlink Ferries to try and ensure that rail tickets from Aberdeen would remain valid if the ferry from Shetland were to be late.

ONLINE TEST

Test yourself on your representatives online at www.brightredbooks.net/N5ModernStudies.

THINGS TO DO AND THINK ABOUT

1 Use their websites to find out about the policies and ideologies of the Green Party or UKIP.

2 Search online for the most up-to-date party manifestos and compare policies in a policy area not shown above.

3 Use the UK Parliament's 'Find Your MP' tool (http://findyourmp.parliament.uk/) to find out who your MP is, or the Scottish Parliament's 'Find Your MSP' tool (http://www.scottish.parliament.uk/help/32438.aspx) to find out who your MSP is.

    Look at their parliamentary and constituency websites to find examples of your MP or MSP working in any of the ways described above in your constituency.

MPs IN PARLIAMENT

DON'T FORGET

constituency = an area which elects an MP; constituents = the people who live in a constituency.

VIDEO LINK

Have a look at this emergency debate from 2011 about phone hacking at the *News of the World* at www.brightredbooks.net/N5ModernStudies. Look how the Speaker, John Bercow, explains the rules of the debate very clearly at the beginning. Labour MP Chris Bryant asked for the debate, so he gets to make the opening statement.

THE WORK OF MPs

The UK Parliament meets at Westminster, London. The main tasks of parliament are to make new laws, and debate and discuss how to make the UK a better place to live.

Concerned citizens may feel an issue is important enough to be brought publicly to their MP's attention. They have the right to go to parliament and tell the MP directly about it. This is called **lobbying**, as they are allowed to approach MPs in the lobby of parliament with these concerns. Lobbying groups or individuals can get a lot of media attention for their cause.

In a typical week MPs meet in the House of Commons from Monday afternoon until Friday afternoon.

It is the main job of MPs to represent their constituents in the House of Commons. This means that MPs can raise the concerns of their constituents and speak up for their points of view. MPs can do this in a number of ways.

DEBATES

Debates are an opportunity for MPs to discuss government policy and current issues, and propose new laws. They allow MPs to voice the concerns and interests of their constituents. They also give MPs a chance to hear different opinions and reach a more balanced point of view.

Debates often get 'lively', so someone has to take charge. In the UK Parliament this person is called the Speaker.

General debates	Adjournment debates	Emergency debates
A general debate is held on a proposal (**motion**) put forward by an MP. These debates have strict rules, enforced by the Speaker. Decisions at the end of a general debate are made by a 'division' (vote).	These are general debates that MPs do not have to vote on. They allow backbench MPs the chance to bring their constituents' concerns to the attention of the House. There is a half-hour debate at the end of each day's sitting.	When a serious issue catches an MP's attention, they can ask the Speaker to grant an emergency debate in which MPs can discuss the issue. The Speaker rarely grants these.

This is the division bell in St Stephen's Tavern next to the Palace of Westminster.

DIVISIONS (VOTES)

When a **division** is called by the Speaker, the division bell rings throughout parliament (and in two pubs nearby!) to call MPs to vote: they have 8 minutes to get to the chamber and vote.

MPs vote by leaving the Commons chamber and going to either the 'Aye' (yes) lobby or the 'No' lobby. Their vote is officially counted as they re-enter the chamber.

Before deciding which way to vote, MPs have to balance what their constituents think, their party's policy and their own opinion. These points of view may be very different!

QUESTION TIME

Question Time takes place every Monday to Thursday for an hour. It gives MPs a chance to ask government ministers about any issues that are their responsibility. For example, if an MP had a question about the military, they could ask the Defence Secretary.

contd

MPs must submit their questions in advance, but can ask a supplementary (extra, follow-on) question after the minister has answered.

Prime Minister's Question Time

Prime Minister's Question Time (PMQs) takes place from 12 noon to 12:30pm every Wednesday when parliament is in session. PMQs always starts with the open question: Question 1: *'If the Prime Minister has any engagements for the rest of the day.'* Following the answer, the MP then asks their supplementary question about an issue they or their constituents feel is important.

The Leader of the Opposition then follows up on this or another topic. They are permitted to ask a total of six questions. The Leader of the Opposition is the only MP who is allowed to come back with further questions.

In theory, the Prime Minister will not know what supplementary questions will be asked of them. However, the Prime Minister will be prepared for likely questions by government departments.

ONLINE

Use BBC Democracy Live (www.brightredbooks.net/N5ModernStudies) to find a recent example of Prime Minister's Questions. What sort of issues are being discussed?

COMMITTEES

In the Houses of Parliament much of the work is done in committees. It is the main job of the committees to scrutinise (keep a close eye on) how the government is doing. Committees are made up of 10–50 MPs (and Lords in some cases) from more than one of the parties in parliament.

General Committees consider Bills (proposed laws) and come up with any changes they think should be made to them. A General Committee can have between 16 and about 50 members, of which the government always has a majority. The committee will call in expert witnesses to give their opinions or receive their opinions in writing. This is called the committee stage (see pages 16–17).

Select Committees hold inquiries in which they investigate issues that they think are important to the British public. Each Select Committee works on topics relating to a specific government department, e.g. the Defence Committee. Committees can call people to give evidence and to face questions from the committee's members.

Examples of Select Committee membership (July 2013)	
Committee	**Defence**
Total members	12
Conservative	Rt Hon James Arbuthnot MP (Chair) Mr Julian Brazier MP Mr Adam Holloway Penny Mordaunt MP Bob Stewart MP
Labour	Thomas Docherty MP Mr Dai Havard MP Mrs Madeleine Moon MP Ms Gisela Stuart MP Derek Twigg MP
Liberal Democrat	Sir Bob Russell MP
Other	Rt Hon Jeffrey M. Donaldson MP (Democratic Unionist)

Grand Committees give MPs the chance to debate issues affecting their regions. These committees work like the House of Commons chamber, with statements from government ministers and a chance to ask them questions. There is a Grand Committee each for Scotland, Wales and Northern Ireland, and eight Grand Committees for English regions. The Scottish Grand Committee has not met for a number of years, as there have been few Bills affecting only Scotland since the formation of the Scottish Parliament.

MPs can represent their constituents by joining committees that deal with issues their constituents are likely to be interested in.

PRIVATE MEMBERS' BILLS

An MP who is not a government minister can also attempt to make a new law by introducing a **Private Member's Bill**. These are rarely passed, as there is not much of parliament's time to devote to them. However, even if the Bill doesn't get passed by parliament, it can bring attention to the issue.

ONLINE TEST

Take the test on MPs in parliament online at www.brightredbooks.net/N5ModernStudies.

THINGS TO DO AND THINK ABOUT

1 Use the UK Parliament's 'Find Your MP' tool (http://findyourmp.parliament.uk/) to find out who your MP is. Look at their parliamentary and constituency websites to find examples of your MP working to represent you in parliament.

THE HOUSE OF LORDS

MEMBERS OF THE HOUSE OF LORDS

The House of Lords is the second chamber of the UK Parliament. It plays a crucial role in making and shaping laws, and keeping a close eye on the UK Government.

There are around 800 members of the House of Lords. Unlike MPs in the House of Commons, **peers** are not elected by the public. There are three types of members, or peers, in the Lords.

Appointed Peers
Baroness Grey-Thompson Former Paralympian
Lord Sugar Businessman
Lord Lloyd-Webber Composer
(Elected) Hereditary Peers
Lord Borwick Elected July 2013
Viscount Ridley Elected February 2013
Bishops
Justin Welby Archbishop of Canterbury

Life peers

Most members of the Lords are life peers, appointed by the Queen. They are recommended by an independent organisation called the Appointments Commission. The Appointments Commission selects people to become peers because of their expertise, knowledge and experience in a specific area, such as science or business. The Commission also tries to 'ensure that the House of Lords represents the diversity of the people of the UK'.

(Elected) hereditary peers

For hundreds of years, the Lords was dominated by hereditary peers. These were peers who inherited their title from a parent, who in turn had inherited it from their parents: the title was passed from generation to generation.

However, this changed in 1999, and the Lords themselves had to vote on which 92 hereditary peers to keep. The rest lost their peerages. When these elected hereditary members pass away or leave the house, the other Lords will vote for another former hereditary peer to replace them. Hereditary peers have become another type of life peer.

Church of England bishops

The third type of peer is made up of 26 bishops from the Church of England. The Archbishop of Canterbury is the most famous of these. The bishops keep their peerage as long as they stay in their position: if they retire or leave the church, their peerage passes on.

There are peers of many different religions in the House of Lords, but the Church of England is the only one that has official representation.

GROUPS OF LORDS

Peers sit in four different groups: government, opposition, **cross-benchers** and bishops. Government peers are peers that are members of whatever party or parties make up the government at that time. Opposition peers are peers who are members of any other parties.

Cross-benchers are peers who were appointed because of their expertise or experience, and don't belong to any party. The bishops aren't members of a party either. As there are so many cross-benchers, the government nearly always has a minority of peers.

The person who is in charge of the running of the House of Lords is called the Lord Speaker. Unlike the Speaker of the House of Commons, the Lord Speaker cannot ask members to be quiet, instead the Lords is self-regulating (the peers look after themselves).

Instead of having a grand chair like in the House of Commons, the Lord Speaker sits on a big cushion-like chair called the woolsack.

The woolsack

ROLES OF THE HOUSE OF LORDS

The House of Lords is independent of the House of Commons, but the two chambers work together to make, pass and shape the laws that affect the whole of the UK. The Lords has three main roles: making laws, considering laws and holding government to account.

Making laws

Members of the House of Lords can introduce Private Members' Bills in the same way that MPs can. If the Bill is supported by an MP, it continues in the Commons (see pages 16–17). Similarly to MPs' Private Members' Bills, it is highly unlikely that Private Members' Bills from the Lords will be granted much time in the Commons.

Considering laws

Around half of the time in the House of Lords is spent considering Bills. The House of Commons and the Lords have to examine every Bill before it can become a law. The Lords plays a crucial role in this process because it allows peers – who do not have to worry about re-election every few years – to add their expert opinion to the law-making process (see pages 16–17). As peerages last a lifetime, the Lords can take a long-term view of any law that is being examined.

Peers may also join Select Committees and help investigate proposed new laws.

Scrutinising government

Members of the Lords play a vital role making laws and keeping a check on (scrutinising) what the UK Government does. They can do this in two main ways: Question Time and debates.

There is a 30-minute question time at the start of business from Monday to Thursday. Peers can ask a government spokesperson up to four initial questions, and then supplementary questions, in each of these. Lords can also submit questions to the government in writing.

In debates, peers add their considerable experience to the discussion of government proposals.

 FACT

Since the Parliament Act 1949 came into force the Lords cannot amend or delay Money Bills (Bills about taxes or public money). Money Bills will receive **Royal Assent** even if the Lords doesn't pass them.

 FACT

Members of the Lords submit about 10,000 written questions to the government annually.

THINGS TO DO AND THINK ABOUT

1   Use the House of Lords website (http://www.parliament.uk/mps-lords-and-offices/lords/) to make a factfile about a peer:

- What sort of peer are they (life, elected hereditary, bishop)?

- When did they join the Lords?

- What group do they belong to (government, opposition, cross-bench)?

- What expertise or experience do they add to the Lords?

2   Use the House of Lords website (http://www.parliament.uk/mps-lords-and-offices/lords/composition-of-the-lords/) to find out the current number, types and parties of peers in the House of Lords.

3   Who do you think should be made a peer? Write a letter to the Appointments Commission, recommending someone for a peerage:

- What skills or expertise would they add to the Lords?

- Why are they the best person that the Appointments Commission could consider?

 ONLINE TEST

Take the test on the House of Lords online at www.brightredbooks.net/N5ModernStudies.

LORDS REFORM?

ARGUMENTS FOR AND AGAINST REFORM

The House of Lords is an extremely controversial part of the UK Parliamentary system. Many people see it as very important that before laws are made, another group of people can give a second opinion on them and that the government's decisions are closely scrutinised.

Many people, however, believe that having a second chamber that is unelected – that the public haven't voted for – is against the principles of **democracy**. These people believe that the House of Lords should either be abolished (got rid of completely) or reformed (changed).

Pros and cons of the current House of Lords

Pros	Cons
Many peers are now extremely experienced in the workings of parliament: to change the system would lose all this expertise.	Important decisions are being made by unelected people who don't have to answer to the public for their decisions through elections.
Not having to worry about re-election, peers can make difficult decisions that may be unpopular in the short term in the long-term interests of the country.	Public opinion should be at the centre of all decisions taken by those in power: it is undemocratic if this is ignored or not taken into account by the Lords.
As it is appointed to give a second opinion, it is clear that the Commons is the main decision-making House. Electing the Lords would make this difference unclear.	The Lords votes on nearly all Bills (proposed laws), and such an important function should be left to those who are chosen by the people.
The Appointments Commission is independent and picks the best people for the job; the public may just choose a popular personality if they were voting.	Voters should be able to choose whomever they like to make decisions on their behalf in parliament.
It's worked for a very long time: why change it now?	The Lords has blocked Bills that the public support: maybe it's not working in the public interest?

The Electoral Reform Society – an organisation that wants to change the UK voting and parliamentary systems – says: 'If you hold the power to help decide how Britain is run you should be elected by us, the British public. That's democracy.' They also claim that 79% of the public support reform.

2010: VIEWS OF THE PARTIES

In the run-up to the 2010 general election, all the main parties proposed reform of the House of Lords in their manifestos. The Conservatives wanted 'a mainly-elected second chamber to replace the current House of Lords'. Labour promised, if elected, to hold a referendum (public vote) on having an elected second house. The Liberal Democrats wanted 'to replace the House of Lords with a fully-elected second chamber with considerably fewer members than the current House' and the SNP wanted to 'scrap' the House of Lords completely.

LORDS REFORM SINCE 2010

2010: The coalition agreement

After the 2010 general election, because no party won more than half of all seats in the House of Commons, the Conservative Party joined (formed a coalition) with the Liberal Democrats, to allow the two parties to form a coalition government.

Before this happened, the two parties negotiated and signed a coalition agreement that set out how they would work together, and what they would work towards.

contd

This document promised to 'establish a committee to bring forward proposals for a wholly or mainly elected upper chamber on the basis of **proportional representation**. The committee will come forward with a draft motion by December 2010.'

The House of Lords Reform Bill

27 June 2012

The coalition introduced the House of Lords Reform Bill. It proposed that the House of Lords should eventually consist of:

- 360 elected members (elected in batches of 120 every 5 years, with a 15-year term and no re-election)
- 90 appointed members
- up to 12 Lords Spiritual (bishops from the Church of England), and
- any ministerial members (of the government).

This would mean a House of Lords approximately half the size of the current House.

11 July 2012

Two weeks later, the House of Commons had a vote on the second reading of the Bill (see the section 'Making laws in the UK'). The result was 462 votes to 124 in favour of continuing with the Bill. However, the result hid the biggest coalition **rebellion** up to that point: 91 Conservative MPs voted against their own coalition government's plan.

The Bill also only passed this stage when a programme motion, which allotted it time to pass through the House of Commons, was dropped. It was likely that the Bill would have been defeated (lost the vote) if it had contained a programme motion. This was also to give the Conservatives time to persuade their MPs of the benefits of reform.

Liberal Democrat leader and Deputy Prime Minister Nick Clegg said: 'When we return in the autumn to vote on this again, we fully expect the Conservatives to deliver this crucial part of the coalition deal – as we have delivered other coalition policies.'

6 August 2012

Liberal Democrat leader Nick Clegg announced that the reform plans would be abandoned, instead of facing a 'slow death' in the House of Commons. He also said the Conservatives 'broke the coalition contract'. In response, he would tell Liberal Democrat MPs to vote against changes to constituency boundaries, which the Conservatives hoped to have in place before the 2015 election.

Katie Ghose, Chief Executive of the Electoral Reform Society, described the failed attempts at reform: 'Our MPs have squandered consensus, in the name of cheap point scoring and political games. All three parties walked into the last election committed to change. Each party has had an opportunity to break the impasse. Each party has chosen not to.'

 ONLINE TEST

Take the 'Lords reform?' test online at www. brightredbooks.net/ N5ModernStudies.

 THINGS TO DO AND THINK ABOUT

1 Put the quote from Katie Ghose into your own words.

2 Imagine you are a political adviser to the UK Government. You have been asked to write a report about the future of the Lords:

    a Should it remain as it is, be reformed or be abolished?

    b Who should be peers and why? Give at least three examples of current or prospective peers.

    c Why do you think this is the best way forward?

    d Link this back to the policies of each party to make your proposal as appealing as possible to all parties: be sure that the government won't repeat the failure of 2012!

MAKING LAWS IN THE UK

THE ROLE OF WESTMINSTER

The UK Parliament makes all laws for England and laws for the whole UK about reserved matters. Introducing **legislation** (laws) also gives individual MPs, or groups of MPs, the chance to represent their constituents' concerns: trying to pass laws about issues that concern them. The first step in making a new law is to propose a **Bill**: a draft law.

TYPES OF BILLS

There are a number of different types of Bills, each given a different name depending on who introduced it. Some of these are given below.

Public Bills

Public Bills change the laws that affect every member of the public in the general population. These are the most common type of Bill. These are normally introduced by government ministers, but sometimes by other MPs or Lords, when they are known as Private Members' Bills.

Private Members' Bills

For an MP who is not in the government to introduce a Private Member's Bill, the MP must do one of three things. First, the ballot is a system in which all MPs applying for a Bill are drawn at random at the start of the parliamentary year. Usually, the first seven selected are timetabled to get a day's debate each. Because they are guaranteed this time, these Bills have the best chance of becoming law.

Second, there is the 10-minute rule. This gives MPs the chance to speak about an issue for up to 10 minutes. This gives MPs the opportunity of seeing if their idea for a Bill would have much support in the Commons.

Finally, there is presentation. Any MP can introduce a Bill into parliament as long as they have officially told the Speaker that they will do so. They are not given the chance to speak in support of their Bill, so these Bills very rarely become law.

Private Bills

Private Bills are Bills that only affect certain organisations, and are for when the organisation is requesting powers that are not the same as the law gives them already. For example, the Canterbury City Council Act 2013 gave council officers the opportunity to seize goods and equipment when they believed an offence had been committed, amongst other things.

Hybrid Bills

Hybrid Bills are Bills that affect the whole population, but have a very significant impact on a specific area of the country, or a specific part of the population, or a specific group. The Bills that were passed to allow the Channel Tunnel to be built are examples of Hybrid Bills.

THE LEGISLATIVE PROCESS

There are a number of stages that a Bill must pass through before it can become a law. Bills beginning in the House of Commons must go through five stages in the Commons before repeating these stages in the Lords. Bills starting in the House of Lords do this in the opposite direction. There is then the consideration of amendments before Royal Assent can be granted, which makes the Bill into an **Act** (law).

DON'T FORGET

Introducing a Bill gives MPs a chance to represent their constituents by highlighting an issue of particular concern to them.

DON'T FORGET

Each Bill must go through multiple stages, in both Houses (Commons and Lords), before it can become a law.

2006	2007	2008	2009	2010	2011	2012
55	31	33	27	41	25	23

Acts of the UK Parliament, 2006–2012.

contd

First reading	The first reading is when the short title of the Bill is read out and its formal place in parliament's timetable is confirmed. There is no debate or discussion.
Second reading	This is also called the debate on the general principles of the Bill. At this stage, the MP responsible for the Bill speaks about why it is needed. Someone from the official Opposition then speaks about the Bill before backbench MPs and other opposition can have their say on it. After they have debated the Bill MPs vote on whether it should continue through parliament.
Committee stage	At this stage, the Bill is examined in detail by a committee of MPs (see page 11). The committee may take evidence from experts and interested groups from outside parliament. The committee may make changes (amendments) to the Bill if members of the committee vote to do so. Every clause (section) in the Bill is agreed to, changed or removed from the Bill by the committee.
Report stage	The report stage of a Bill is when all MPs are given the opportunity to consider making further amendments to it after it has been examined in committee. All MPs may speak and vote on the Bill at this stage or propose amendments. This all takes place in the debating chamber of the House of Commons.
Third reading	This is the last chance for the House of Commons to debate the contents of a Bill. A short debate is had, in which each section of the Bill can be included or not. After this debate, the Commons votes on whether or not to approve the third reading of the Bill.
The other House	After passing the third reading, the Bill is passed to the other House. Bills which started in the House of Commons pass to the House of Lords, and vice versa. The other House then proceeds with all the same stages up to this point.
Consideration of amendments	After both Houses have passed the Bill through its third reading, the Bill returns to the House it came from, with any amendments made by the other House. Before the Bill can pass this stage, both Houses have to agree on the exact wording of the Bill. This can cause the Bill to 'ping pong' between the Houses while amendments are agreed upon. On very rare occasions, where the Houses cannot agree on amendments, the Bill fails.
Royal Assent	This is the final stage, where the monarch agrees to make the Bill an Act (law). It is now a formality: it happens automatically.

CASE STUDY: SUNBEDS (REGULATION) ACT 2010

The Bill for this Act was introduced by then Cardiff North MP Julie Morgan on 16 December 2009. She had won the ballot. The Bill would affect England and Wales, and aimed to ban under-18s from using tanning salons and automatic coin-operated salons.

At its second reading on 29 January 2010, Julie Morgan MP said: 'The Bill is very important, as the intention is to protect young people.'

In the committee stage, the Bill was given cross-party support and was passed without amendment on 10 February 2010. The report and third reading stages in the Commons happened on 12 March 2010.

The Bill passed through the Lords' first, second and third readings on 15 March, 30 March and 8 April 2010, respectively. The Sunbeds (Regulation) Bill received Royal Assent and became the Sunbed (Regulation) Act 2010 on 8 April 2010. It came into force in England and Wales on 8 April 2011.

FACT

Royal Assent was last refused in 1707, when Queen Anne refused a Bill on settling the militia in Scotland.

VIDEO LINK

Watch the video from the UK Parliament website which explains the whole process at www.brightredbooks.net/N5ModernStudies.

ONLINE TEST

Take the UK legislative process test online at www.brightredbooks.net/N5ModernStudies.

ONLINE

Head to the BrightRED Digital Zone for a great activity about Passing a Private Members' Bill!

THINGS TO DO AND THINK ABOUT

1 Research and makes notes on a Bill the UK Parliament is looking at just now, using the UK Parliament's 'Bills before Parliament' page: http://services.parliament.uk/bills/.

   a What type of Bill is it? Who introduced it?

   b What does it hope to achieve?

   c What stage is it at?

2 Do the same for a recent Act of the UK Parliament (see http://www.parliament.uk/business/bills-and-legislation/current-bills/previous-bills/).

   a Present the Act to the class.

MSPs IN PARLIAMENT 1

THE WORK OF MSPs

The Scottish Parliament meets in Edinburgh to make decisions about devolved matters. The main tasks of the Scottish Parliament are to make new laws, and debate and discuss how to make Scotland a better place to live.

MSPs are usually in parliament for at least three days of the week: Tuesdays, Wednesdays and Thursdays. Parliament is in session (meets) for around 35 weeks per year. When it is not meeting, parliament is in recess.

Concerned citizens may feel an issue is important enough to be brought publicly to their MSP's attention. They have the right to go to parliament and tell the MSP directly about it. This is called lobbying, as they are allowed to approach MSPs in the lobby of parliament with these concerns. Lobbying groups or individuals can get a lot of media attention for their cause.

An MSP's main job is to represent their constituents in the Scottish Parliament. This means that MSPs can raise the concerns of the constituents and speak up for their point of view. MSPs can do this in a number of ways.

DEBATES

Debates are an opportunity for MSPs to discuss government policy and current issues, and propose new laws. MSPs can put forward motions about problems their constituents have raised and can ask parliament to consider how to solve them.

They also give MSPs a chance to hear different opinions and reach a more balanced point of view.

Debates often get 'lively', so someone has to take charge. In the Scottish Parliament, this person is called the **Presiding Officer**. He/she is an elected MSP who is voted in to this important and impartial role by the other MSPs.

contd

General debates

General debates are plenary (summing up) debates held on a proposal (**motion**) put forward by an MSP, usually a minister or Cabinet secretary.

These debates have strict rules, and it is the Presiding Officer's job to enforce these. At the start of the debate, the Presiding Officer says: 'Members who wish to take part in the debate should press the Request to Speak button now.' This allows the Presiding Officer to work out (and remind the MSPs) how much time each MSP can speak for in the debate.

General debates give MSPs a chance to represent their constituents by making points that reflect their point of view. There are not always votes at the end of a general debate.

Members' business debates

Members' business debates are an opportunity for an MSP to represent their constituents by raising a local issue or bringing up a certain event to which the Scottish Parliament may not otherwise devote time to discuss. Only MSPs who are not a Cabinet secretary or minister are allowed to propose motions during members' business debates. For example, on 21 March 2013, Angus MacDonald, MSP for Falkirk East, introduced a motion on '75 Years of Young Farmers Clubs in Scotland' in a members' business debate.

These debates happen after Decision Time on Wednesdays and Thursdays, and last for up to 45 minutes.

Emergency debates

When a serious issue comes to the Presiding Officer's attention, he/she can grant an emergency debate in which MSPs can discuss the issue. These are rarely granted.

In August 2009, the Presiding Officer granted an emergency debate so that the Cabinet Secretary for Justice, Kenny MacAskill, could issue a statement and answer questions about his decision to release the convicted Lockerbie bomber Abdelbaset Ali Mohmed al-Megrahi. In his opening statement, the Presiding Officer said: 'This topic is of the utmost seriousness, and the eyes of many people around the globe are on the parliament today.'

DIVISIONS (VOTES)

When the parliament must make a decision, for example about a Bill, a division is called by the Presiding Officer. Most of the divisions are held at **Decision Time**, at 5pm on Tuesdays to Thursdays, and 12 noon on Fridays.

A division bell rings throughout the parliament to tell MSPs to go to the chamber to vote. In the Scottish Parliament, MSPs vote by pressing a button on their electronic consoles. There are three voting options: 'Yes', 'No' and 'Abstain' (choose not to vote).

Before deciding which way to vote, MSPs have to balance what their constituents think, their party's policy and their own opinion. These points of view may be very different!

Scottish Parliament voting console.

ONLINE TEST

Take the MSPs in parliament test online at www. brightredbooks.net/ N5ModernStudies.

MSPs IN PARLIAMENT 2

QUESTION TIME

There are different forms of Question Time which take place in the Scottish Parliament. MSPs are given the opportunity to ask questions that are of great interest to them or to represent their constituents by asking questions about an issue that concerns them.

First Minister's Question Time

First Minister's Question Time (FMQs) takes place for half an hour every week, usually on Thursdays at noon. The other MSPs, in particular the leaders of the opposition parties, have the chance to ask the First Minister questions about decisions that the government has made or plans to make.

FMQs is where it is possible to see MSPs at their most rowdy and badly behaved: shouting over each other and making cheeky remarks. The Presiding Officer is required to keep the peace!

FMQs starts with the open question: *'To ask the First Minister what engagements he has planned for the rest of the day.'* Following the answer, the MSP then asks their real question about a current issue.

The Leader of the Opposition then follows up on this or another topic. The other parties are allocated questions according to their share of MSPs in the parliament.

In theory, the First Minister will not know what questions will be asked. However, the First Minister will be prepared for likely questions by government departments.

Topical Question Time

This normally takes place on a Tuesday and allows MSPs to ask questions about issues that have very recently happened, but that parliament hasn't discussed yet.

Portfolio (General) Question Time

Portfolio Question Time is when MSPs are given the chance to ask Cabinet secretaries and ministers questions about the policy area they are responsible for. For example, MSPs can ask the Minister for Public Health questions about health and wellbeing in Scotland.

This usually takes place on a Wednesday, for around half an hour.

VIDEO LINK

Watch the latest FMQs at www.brightredbooks.net/N5ModernStudies.

COMMITTEES

Who sits where?

Typical seating arrangements at a committee meeting

Deputy Convener · Convener · Clerk · Official Reporters · Witnesses · MSPs · Broadcasting · Journalists and public

Committees play a vital role in the work of the Scottish Parliament. The Scottish Parliament is unicameral (has only one house or level, without the equivalent of the House of Lords in the UK Parliament), so the committees are even more important than they are in the UK Parliament.

The Scottish Parliament has different types of committee (mandatory and subject) and can form new ones if specific issues or Bills need to be considered. Each committee is involved in a certain policy area or areas.

contd

Mandatory committees are committees that must exist in every session of the Scottish Parliament (between each Scottish Parliament election). These cover topics such as equal opportunities, finance and public petitions.

Subject committees are formed at the start of, or during, a session (after each Scottish Parliament election) and are formed to look at a group of policy or subject areas until the next election. An example is the Referendum Bill Committee, which was set up in October 2012 to examine and prepare for the 2014 referendum on Scottish independence.

The membership of committees is usually between 5 and 15 members, and is supposed to roughly reflect the balance of parties in parliament: the more MSPs a party has the more MSPs it should have in each committee.

Selected committees and membership July 2013		
Committee	**Equal Opportunities Committee**	**Referendum Bill Committee**
Type	Mandatory	Subject
Membership	7	11
SNP	Marco Biagi (Deputy Convener) Christian Allard John Mason	Bruce Crawford (Convener) Annabelle Ewing Linda Fabiani Rob Gibson Stewart Maxwell Stuart McMillan
Labour	Mary Fee (Convener) Siobhan McMahon	James Kelly (Deputy Convener) Patricia Ferguson
Conservative	Alex Johnstone	Annabel Goldie
Liberal Democrat		Tavish Scott
Other	John Finnie (Independent)	Patrick Harvie (Green Party)

Committees usually meet once a week or fortnightly, on a Tuesday, Wednesday or Thursday morning. These meetings are held in public so that journalists and ordinary citizens can see what discussions the committees are having.

Committees are heavily involved in scrutinising (investigating closely) the laws that government or MSPs want to make (see Chapter 9), and do this to make sure that the decisions made are the best possible results for Scotland. One way they can do this by inviting witnesses (including Cabinet secretaries and ministers) to speak and answer questions about the issues being examined. For example, in January and February 2013, the Referendum Bill Committee welcomed officials from Jersey, Guernsey and the Isle of Man to give evidence on how they each changed the way their elections run to give the vote to 16- and 17-year-olds. Committees also go on fact-finding missions to the areas affected to gather first-hand evidence.

PRIVATE MEMBERS' BILLS

Any MSP who is not a member of the government can also try to introduce a Member's Bill to parliament (see pages 22–23). This Bill could be about an issue that constituents feel strongly about or that affects the area the MSP represents.

ONLINE TEST

Take the MSPs in parliament test online at www. brightredbooks.net/ N5ModernStudies.

THINGS TO DO AND THINK ABOUT

Use the Scottish Parliament's 'Find Your MSP' tool (http://www.scottish.parliament. uk/help/32438.aspx) to find out who your MSP is. Look at their parliamentary and constituency websites to find examples of your MSP working to represent you in all different ways.

MAKING LAWS IN SCOTLAND

The Scottish Parliament passes laws about devolved matters when MSPs feel that a law will make Scotland a better place. Introducing legislation (laws) also gives individual MSPs, or groups of MSPs, the chance to represent their constituents' concerns, passing laws about issues that concern them. The first step in making a new law is to propose a Bill: a draft law.

TYPES OF BILLS

There are a number of different types of Bills, each given a different name depending on who introduced them. Some of these are given below.

Executive (Government) Bills

These are Bills introduced by the Cabinet secretary – government official – who is in charge of the policy area that the Bill falls under. For example, the Justice Secretary could introduce Bills to change the ways the police or courts operate.

Members' Bills

These are Bills introduced by an MSP who is not a member of the government. To introduce a Member's Bill to parliament, the proposal needs to be supported by 18 other MSPs from at least half of the parties in parliament. The Bill must also be different to any Bills the government plans to introduce.

Committee Bills

Conveners (leaders) of Scottish Parliament committees (see pages 20–21) can introduce Bills related to their committee's policy area. For example, the Education and Culture Committee can introduce a Bill about the way that schools operate.

Private Bills

Private Bills are Bills that give a person or organisation particular powers or benefits that are greater than the law would normally allow. These are dealt with in a different way to the Bills above, as are Hybrid Bills.

Hybrid Bills

Hybrid Bills are Bills that affect some more than others. They are usually to do with planning or development projects. The first one considered by the Scottish Parliament was to allow a new crossing for the River Forth.

DON'T FORGET

Introducing a Bill gives MSPs a chance to represent their constituents by highlighting an issue of particular concern to their constituents.

THE LEGISLATIVE PROCESS

There are a number of stages that a Bill must pass through before it can become a law. These occur in four main stages.

Stage 1

When a government or Member's Bill is proposed, the relevant committee will conduct an inquiry into the proposal. They will investigate possible effects of the Bills, including hearing evidence from expert witnesses. The committee will publish a report on what it finds (Committee Bills miss this stage out).

The parliament then has a short debate and vote on the general principles of the Bill. This just means that the MSPs think it is worth the parliament's time to consider. If MSPs don't agree to these principles, the Bill fails. If they agree, it passes on to the next stage.

contd

Stage 2

In stage 2, the relevant committee looks at the proposed Bill in great detail. This stage is called detailed consideration. The committee can make changes, or amendments, to the Bill at this stage.

Stage 3

The amended Bill is then passed to the whole Scottish Parliament for discussion. MSPs can make further amendments to the Bill at this stage. MSPs then vote on the Bill. If less than half (a minority) of MSPs vote in favour of the Bill, it fails. If more than half (a majority) vote in favour, it moves to the next stage.

After stage 3

After the Scottish Parliament has voted in favour of a Bill, the Secretary of State for Scotland and a legal expert called the Advocate General for Scotland (both UK Government officials) have 4 weeks to decide if they object to the law because it interferes with the UK's national security or is not a decision the Scottish Parliament has the power to make. If they propose changes, the Bill must be reconsidered in the Scottish Parliament.

Usually there are no objections at this stage, and the Bill is passed to the monarch for Royal Assent, when the Queen officially signs the Bill into law.

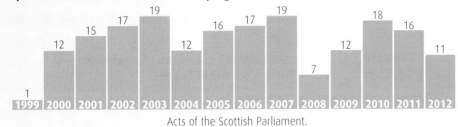

Acts of the Scottish Parliament.

CASE STUDY: SCOTTISH REGISTER OF TARTANS ACT 2008

This Bill was introduced by Jamie McGrigor MSP on 25 March 2008. The Bill aimed to establish a register of tartans.

In stage 1, on 6 June 2008, the Economy, Energy and Tourism Committee recommended that the parliament agree to the general principles of the Bill. On 19 June, the Scottish Parliament agreed to the general principles.

In stage 2, there was one minor amendment from Jamie McGrigor MSP about the definition of tartan. The Bill passed stage 2 on 10 September 2008.

The stage 3 debate was held on 9 October 2008. The Bill passed at Decision Time.

The Bill received Royal Assent and became the Scottish Register of Tartans Act on 13 November 2008.

 THINGS TO DO AND THINK ABOUT

1 Research and makes notes on a Bill the Scottish Parliament is looking at just now using the Scottish Parliament's 'Current Bills' page: http://www.scottish.parliament.uk/parliamentarybusiness/Bills/576.aspx.

   a What type of Bill is it? Who introduced it?

   b What does it hope to achieve?

   c What stage is it at?

   d Present the Act to the class.

2 Do the same for a recent Act of the Scottish Parliament: http://www.scottish.parliament.uk/parliamentarybusiness/Bills/610.aspx.

LOCAL COUNCILS

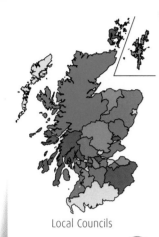

Local Councils

THE PROVISION OF SERVICES

Local councils (or local authorities) are responsible for providing services in their local area, such as education, leisure and public transport.

There are 32 local authorities in Scotland, ranging in population from under 20,000 in Orkney to over 600,000 in Glasgow, and in size from 26 square miles in Dundee to 12,437 square miles in the Highlands.

Each local authority area is run by a council. Local residents elect councillors to represent them in the council, usually every 4 years. Local councillors are elected using the single transferable vote system (see pages 34–35). Three or four councillors are elected to represent a specific area, called a **ward**. The work of local councillors is discussed on pages 26–27.

FUNDING

Local councils get most (around 85%) of their money in a block grant from the Scottish Government. The rest of their money comes from:

- grants for **capital expenditure**: the Scottish Government often gives local authorities money for expensive projects, like new schools or bridges

- non-domestic rates: local taxes on businesses

- **council tax**: paid on each residential property (house or flat), roughly based on its value.

COUNCIL SERVICES

Each local authority is responsible for providing services in their area. There are three main types of services:

- mandatory services: these are services that the law says local councils have to provide, such as education and social work

- permissive services: councils do not have to provide these, but usually choose to, such as leisure centres

- discretionary services: councils may choose to give money to specific programmes.

Councils also have regulatory powers. This means awarding health and safety certificates to restaurants and take-aways, planning permission for building works, and licences to taxis, bars and nightclubs.

Local councils make their own decisions and officially only have to answer to the people (and voters) in their area. However, there are examples of the Scottish Government influencing the decisions of local councils. Some of these are discussed in the case studies below.

CASE STUDIES

Edinburgh trams

Transport is a devolved issue, and is also an issue under local authority control. In 2002, Transport Initiatives Edinburgh (now called 'Tie') was formed to look at long-term transport for the city. It concluded that congestion was going to become a big problem in future, as Edinburgh's population is predicted to increase. A bus-only public transport network would not be enough.

The original planned tram network was predicted to cost £498m, and go from Newbridge and Edinburgh Airport down to Leith and Crewe Toll in the north-east of the city. It was due to be completed by summer 2011.

In June 2007, the Scottish Parliament voted to provide a maximum of £500m to City of Edinburgh Council for this capital expenditure project. In July 2007, the first works on the tram lines took place in Leith. There were a number of problems in the early stages of construction, including contract disputes, and the costs began to rise significantly.

By 2011, plans for a wider tram network had been shelved (stopped). Instead, the trams would be on one line, from the airport into the city. On 25 August 2011, City of Edinburgh Council held a vote on whether to stop the trams at Haymarket, in the west of the city, rather than continuing to St Andrew Square, in the centre. The vote passed. City of Edinburgh Council had decided that the trams should stop at Haymarket station.

Five days later, on 30 August 2011, Finance Secretary John Swinney said that the Scottish Government would not pay its final payment of £72m, as the plans had changed too much. This Scottish Government decision forced City of Edinburgh Council to have another vote, and on 2 September 2011, the vote passed 28/15 in favour of continuing to St Andrew Square. The trams are now planned to finish in 2014, at a cost of £776m.

DON'T FORGET

Capital expenditure is usually funded with a large Scottish Government grant.

Trump golf course

In 2006, US multimillionaire Donald Trump announced plans to build a new golf centre, costing up to £1bn, with two courses, a hotel and a holiday home complex, on the Menie Estate in Aberdeenshire. The First Minister of the time, Jack (now Lord) McConnell, met Mr Trump twice at this stage. This caused concern amongst some, with a Green Party spokesperson saying: 'Mr McConnell is clearly backing this project but it's actually a job for the local council to decide and not him.'

Groups such as Scottish Natural Heritage, the Royal Society for the Protection of Birds (RSPB) and Sustainable Aberdeenshire also raised concerns about the damage that the course could do to the local scenery and bird populations.

In September 2007, a local council area committee deferred (put off until later) a decision on planning permission for the golf course. In November 2007, the plan was rejected by Aberdeenshire councillors. On 4 December 2007, SNP Finance Minister John Swinney 'called in' the application, which meant the government would have the final say on the matter. First Minister Alex Salmond had controversially met members of the Trump Organisation the day before, but said that he did this because it was part of his job as a local MSP (see Chapter 7).

In November 2008, the Scottish Government approved the golf resort. The first golf course opened in July 2012.

THINGS TO DO AND THINK ABOUT

1 Make a list of all the ways you have used council services in the past week. How important is the local council to your daily life?

2 Write a summary (two or three paragraphs) of each of the case studies above. What do they tell us about the power that local councils have compared to those of the Scottish Government?

WORK OF LOCAL COUNCILLORS

FACT

The biggest Scottish council is Glasgow City Council, with 79 councillors. The smallest is Orkney, with 21 councillors.

THE COMPOSITION OF LOCAL COUNCILS

Local councils are made up of elected councillors. There are 1223 councillors in total in Scotland. Each **ward**, or area, elects three or four councillors. They are elected using the single transferable vote system (see pages 34–35).

Councillors earn a basic salary of £15,452, or more if they are an opposition spokesperson or are the convener of a committee (see below). Council leaders can earn up to £51,508 per year, depending on the size of their local authority.

Councillors have a number of main roles that they must fulfil in order to provide local solutions for local problems. Malcolm Bell, Convener of Shetland Islands Council (SIC), puts it like this:

'My personal belief is that decision making (and the ability to fund and be accountable for such decisions) should be devolved to the lowest possible level. There is a great deal of evidence that good decisions are made in this environment ... Local authorities need the freedom to provide local services according to the situation pertaining in their area. One size does not fit all.'

Convener Malcolm Bell.

SURGERIES

Councillors are elected by voters to represent their concerns and opinions when important local decisions are made. In order to learn about their constituents' concerns, councillors hold **surgeries**. These are open meetings where any resident can meet their councillor and raise any issues they feel strongly about or ask questions about what the council is doing. Nick Cook, councillor for Liberton/Gilmerton in Edinburgh, holds surgeries three times a month in different places around his ward. Councillors can then represent their constituents by raising these concerns within the council or at a higher level.

Councillor Nick Cook.

FULL COUNCIL MEETINGS

Many important council decisions are taken by a meeting of the full council. These meetings occur when the entire council meets together to make decisions about what to do in their area. Decisions are made by voting. When voting, councillors don't just base their decisions on their own opinion, but also what their party wants and the views that they have heard from their constituents, for example at surgeries.

Meetings are held according to that council's rules. For example, the City of Edinburgh Council usually meets once a month. Full council meetings are open to the public so anyone can attend and watch decisions being made. The **agenda** and **minutes** (written record) of council meetings are made available to the public.

COMMITTEES

Paul Godzik.

Local councillors may also join council committees. These are small groups of councillors who propose new decisions for the council or scrutinise (closely examine) decisions the council has already made. Each committee works on a different topic or policy area. For example, the City of Edinburgh Council has an Education, Children and Families Committee. Its convener (leader) is Councillor Paul Godzik.

If a local resident has a complaint or wants to raise an issue about this topic area, they can contact a member of this committee even if they are not from that councillor's area.

DELIVERING SERVICES

As well as committees, councillors can also be involved in arm's-length external organisations (ALEOs). These are organisations outside the council that the council can use to deliver services like leisure services, property maintenance, transport or economic development. At this time of budget cuts, councils are beginning to use ALEOs more, as using them can often be cheaper than using the council's own departments.

Councillors may also be appointed to sit on a Joint Board. These boards are responsible for overseeing the delivery of council services. Councillors from City of Edinburgh, Fife, Perth and Kinross and West Lothian Councils sit on the Forth Estuary Transport Authority, which is responsible for the maintenance and operation of the Forth Road Bridge.

Forth Road Bridge.

WORKING WITH OTHER REPRESENTATIVES

In order to make the best decisions possible, local councillors often meet with other representatives. Councillors might meet with community councillors, MSPs or MPs if they think this will help to resolve the issue. For example, if a constituent raised a concern about health care in their ward, their councillor could discuss the issue with the area's MSPs and ask them to raise it in the Scottish Parliament.

CELEBRATING LOCAL SUCCESSES

Local councillors are, of course, primarily concerned with very local issues. As well as providing services and fixing problems, councils are also very keen to celebrate achievements or efforts made by people in the local area.

Shetland Islands Council Convener Malcolm Bell presents Diamond Jubilee certificates and badges to Shetland's School Crossing Patrol Officers.

THINGS TO DO AND THINK ABOUT

1   Find out who your local councillor is using your council's webpage.

2   Try to find examples of your local councillors working in each of the ways described above.

 Use what you find to make an A4 poster called 'The work of local councillors'.

3   How important do you think local councils are in Scotland?

 Use what you have learned about the parliament and local councils to write a report explaining what you think.

ONLINE TEST

Take the test on local councillors at www.brightredbooks.net/N5ModernStudies.

ELECTIONS AND ELECTION CAMPAIGNS

REPRESENTATIVE DEMOCRACY

The UK is a **representative democracy**. This means that the people have power (democracy) and that they choose people to speak up for them when important decisions are made (representatives).

These representatives are voted in by their constituents in elections. This means that every few years, the public get a chance to choose who to send to council or parliament to make decisions for them. Before these election days, there is a set period of time in which the **candidates** and their parties can campaign to attempt to win votes: **election campaigns**.

WHY HAVE ELECTION CAMPAIGNS?

Election campaigns perform a number of functions in a democracy.

First, they tell the public about the candidates' policies. The **electorate** (voters) will have a choice of people to vote for in the election, so the parties and candidates spend a lot of time and effort telling the electorate what they stand for.

Second, election campaigns highlight local concerns to candidates. Election campaigns give the public a chance to speak face to face with candidates, who will learn a lot over this time about what the electorate see as the really important issues in their area. These may be very different from the policies or priorities of the candidate's party.

Third, election campaigns give candidates and parties in power the chance to highlight their achievements since the last election. Candidates want re-election (to be voted in again) and so will do everything they can to make sure that the electorate know about all of their achievements in the role.

Equally, election campaigns give opposing candidates and parties the chance to highlight the candidate's or party in power's failures since the last election. This is called **negative campaigning**.

During these periods, politics is given more coverage in the media, for example in **party election broadcasts** (see pages 40–41) and many people begin discussing politics more.

STANDING AS A CANDIDATE

Those who are particularly committed to making their local area a better place to live may choose to stand as a candidate in an election. People may stand as an independent candidate or for a party. Depending on the type of election, one or more candidate per party can stand for election in an area.

Standing as a candidate is a considerable time commitment. Candidates spend time **canvassing** the voters in their area. This means going door-to-door, introducing themselves to prospective voters, explaining policies and listening to the concerns of voters.

Candidates also appear in the media, attempting to show themselves and their policies in a good light. For example, a candidate for a local council election may write a letter to the local newspaper, while a candidate for a parliamentary seat may try to get on a regional TV news bulletin. The local area may hold a **hustings**, a public event where the candidates give speeches and are asked questions about themselves and their policies.

Canvassing voters

Personal qualities of candidates

Potential candidates are trying to appeal to voters to choose them over the other candidates. Voters are usually more likely to vote for candidates they

contd

see as trustworthy, honest, qualified for and capable of doing the job, and hardworking. Being a confident public speaker is also extremely useful. There are, however, a number of characteristics that seem to help people get elected. Successfully elected candidates (like MPs and MSPs) are much more likely than the electorate to be male, white, middle-aged, university graduates and reasonably wealthy.

PARTICIPATING IN ELECTION CAMPAIGNS

Without standing as a candidate, there are many ways that members of the public can participate in an election campaign.

Joining a political party

By joining a political party members of the public can share their point of view and help their party come up with policies that fit with many members' views. To join a party, a membership fee must be paid and the money that parties raise this way can contribute a great deal towards paying the costs of a campaign. Members (or non-members) can also donate to a campaign whenever they want. Members of parties can also accompany or assist their party/candidate when canvassing.

Non-party members

Without joining a party, the public can participate in election campaigns by publicising a supported party or candidate. This can be done through putting up posters in windows, handing out leaflets containing policies, or putting up signs in the garden or on lampposts. Of course, party members can also do this. Members of the public can attend hustings to learn more about the different candidates standing in their area. They can raise concerns that they have, knowing that the candidates will have to respond then and there.

People can also become more educated about the candidates and parties standing for election. Watching party election broadcasts (see pages 40–41) on TV or reading election leaflets and election coverage in the newspapers will mean that on election day the voter will be sure to make a reasoned decision. To help voters do this, each party publishes a manifesto, a document that contains all their policies.

WHY IS IT IMPORTANT TO VOTE?

Elections are the time, every few years, when the public gets to choose the people who will make the decisions that affect us all every day. Once elected, representatives have a **mandate** (power and right) to make these important decisions. It is therefore crucially important that the people voted into power reflect the opinions of the public.

Those who chose not to vote may not be happy with the decisions their representatives make, but they have lost their right to complain if they didn't help inform the electoral process by voting.

Voting is a democratic right. As with all rights, it comes with a responsibility: in this case to use it. It is not a right that everyone in Scotland has always had, and is one that many people around the world are still fighting and dying for, such as in the Arab Spring (see pages 102–103). Despite this, many people do not bother to vote in Scotland in the UK. This is called apathy. The **turnout** (percentage of people who could vote who actually do) is lower than you might think.

THINGS TO DO AND THINK ABOUT

1 Find at least three parties' manifestos online. Compare the policies each party has in a certain area, e.g. tax.
2 Watch some party election broadcasts on YouTube. What sort of pictures and words do they use to convince you to vote for them?
3 Imagine you are a candidate standing in an election. Prepare the introductory speech you would use when canvassing.

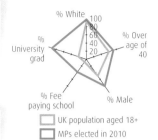

MPs' characteristics differ from those of the population they serve.

FACT

Each of the main political parties has different membership fees depending on your circumstances (like if you're a student). The basic rates (2013) are:

Conservative	£25
Labour	£44.50
Liberal Democrat	£12
SNP	£12

FACT

Turnout in recent elections

UK general election 2010	65%
Scottish Parliament election 2011	50%
Scottish local council elections 2012	40%

ONLINE TEST

Take the test on elections and election campaigns at www.brightredbooks.net/ N5ModernStudies.

FIRST PAST THE POST

UK parliamentary map

Isle of Wight: Constituency with largest electorate: 110,900.

Na h-Eileanan an Iar: Constituency with smallest electorate: 21,985.

THE IMPORTANCE OF CONSTITUENCIES

The **First Past The Post** (FPTP) voting system is used to elect MPs to the UK Parliament. For these elections, the UK is divided up into 650 constituencies (areas which elect a representative):

- 533 in England
- 59 in Scotland
- 40 in Wales
- 18 in Northern Ireland.

Constituency sizes and populations can be very different, but the average number of voters in each constituency (electorate) is approximately 71,000. Each constituency elects one MP.

Boundary changes

Before the 2010 UK general election, both the Conservatives and the Liberal Democrats wanted to reduce the number of MPs. The Conservatives wanted 600, while the Liberal Democrats wanted 500 (elected under a different system). One reason for this is to save money: up to £12m a year. They also argued that it would make elections and politics fairer, as each person's vote would count a similar amount.

The coalition government introduced a Bill that proposed dividing the country up differently so that the number of voters in each constituency would be within 5% of 76,641 (exempt would be Na h-Eileanan an Iar, Orkney and Shetland, and the Isle of Wight).

However, after the Conservatives dropped support for the Liberal Democrat policy of House of Lords reform, the Liberal Democrats withdrew support for these boundary changes. In January 2013, the planned redrawing of boundaries was postponed until 2018 at the earliest.

HOW TO VOTE

To vote in an FPTP election, voters get a sheet of paper with the names and parties of all the candidates written on it (a **ballot paper**). There is a maximum of one candidate per party in each constituency. Voters vote for a candidate by placing an 'X' in the box next to their preferred candidate's name.

In each seat, the candidate who gets the most votes (a **plurality** or simple majority) wins. This means that the winning candidate only needs to have one more vote than the candidate who comes second to win.

The closest result in the 2010 UK general election was in Hampstead and Kilburn, when Glenda Jackson of Labour was re-elected with 17,332 votes (32.81%). Her closest rival was just 42 votes behind, with 17,290 votes (32.73%).

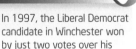

UK general election ballot paper.

FACT

In 1997, the Liberal Democrat candidate in Winchester won by just two votes over his Conservative opponent!

UK general election results 2010 (selected parties)

Party	Number of seats	Number of votes	Seats (%)	Votes (%)
Conservative	307	10,726,614	47.2	36.1
Labour	258	8,609,527	39.7	29
Liberal Democrat	57	6,836,824	8.8	23
Democratic Unionist Party (Northern Ireland)	8	168,216	1.2	0.6
SNP	6	491,386	0.9	1.7
UKIP	0	919,546	0	3.1

contd

FPTP has many advantages and disadvantages. Some of these are summarised below.

Advantages	Disadvantages
FPTP is the simplest voting system to understand for voters: it's how groups make most decisions.	As candidates only need to have a plurality to win, there are a large number of **wasted votes** (votes for a losing candidate) that count for nothing.
The voter is making a clear choice of which candidate they want to win the seat (or the party they want to form the government).	When a voter knows that there are only two candidates likely to win – and they don't support either of these – they may vote for their least-disliked candidate to stop their most-disliked from winning. This is called **tactical voting** and doesn't allow the voter to really express their choice or wishes.
Having one MP per constituency means that voters know who to contact with their problems and who is speaking up for them. This is called having a strong **constituency link**.	There are many seats where one party is incredibly likely to win: these are called **safe seats**. Other parties and candidates spend little time or money campaigning in safe seats, and instead campaign in seats they have a chance of winning, suggesting some votes count for more than others.
It is easy to count the votes and work out the winner: results are quickly found.	FPTP election results are usually very **disproportional** (the share of seats does not fairly represent the share of votes for a party). This often means that smaller parties do not get the number of seats they may deserve, and that votes for these parties are usually wasted votes.
FPTP normally leads to one of the two main parties winning most of the seats and forming a **majority government**. When this happens, they can carry out their policies reasonably quickly and easily.	FPTP doesn't always lead to a majority government. This leads to slower decision making and parties having to make compromises that nobody voted for.

THINGS TO DO AND THINK ABOUT

1   Use the 2010 UK general election results to find examples of the advantages and disadvantages of the first-past-the-post voting system.

2   Find out the name of your constituency and who your MP is using the UK Parliament website: http://findyourmp.parliament.uk/.

3   Use the BBC's 'Constituency List' on their Election 2010 Results page (http://news.bbc. co.uk/1/shared/election2010/results/) to find your constituency's result.

   a   Find out the share of votes your MP won with.

   b   Work out the number of wasted votes in your constituency.

4   Hold a class UK general election!

   ●   Each group will act as a constituency.

   ●   Each member of your group will be representing a candidate from a different political party: Conservative, Labour, Liberal Democrat, SNP, UKIP, etc.

   ●   Copy out the ballot paper, adding your group's name.

   ●   Vote for your preferred candidate by writing an 'X' in the box next to their name.

   ●   Copy and complete the table below using your class election results:

Party	Number of seats	Number of votes	Seats (%)	Votes (%)
Conservative				
Labour				
Liberal Democrat				
SNP				
UKIP				

What do your class results tell you about the first-past-the-post system?

VIDEO LINK

Check out 'BBC Class Clips – FPTP explained using pizza' at www.brightredbooks.net/ N5ModernStudies

ONLINE TEST

Test your knowledge of FPTP online at www. brightredbooks.net/ N5ModernStudies.

THE ADDITIONAL MEMBER SYSTEM

Election of the Scottish Parliament
You have **two** votes

Regional Members	Vote once only (X)	Constituency Member	Vote once only (X)
B Party		C Candidate	
F Party		F Candidate	
G Party		G Candidate	
K Party		N Candidate	
M Party		R Candidate	
S Party		Z Candidate	
T Party			
Y Party			
A Individual Candidate			
E Individual Candidate			
P Individual Candidate			

Scottish Parliament ballot paper.

CONSTITUENCIES AND REGIONS

The **Additional Member System** (AMS) is used to elect MSPs to the Scottish Parliament. For these elections, Scotland is divided up into 73 constituencies and 8 regions. Voters vote twice:

- once for a candidate in their constituency

- once for a party in their region.

Each of these votes is counted a different way to give more **proportional** results than FPTP. Because it mixes two types of voting system to do this, AMS is called a hybrid system.

AMS CONSTITUENCIES

Scottish Parliament constituencies

Under AMS, each constituency elects one constituency MSP using FPTP. Each voter votes for a candidate by placing an 'X' next to the name of their chosen candidate. The candidate with the most votes (a **plurality**) wins. Seventy-three MSPs are elected this way.

Scottish Parliament elections 2011: constituencies scoreboard

Party	Number of seats	Number of votes	Seats (%)	Votes (%)
SNP	53	903,000	73	45.4
Labour	15	630,000	21	31.7
Conservative	3	277,000	4	13.9
Liberal Democrat	2	158,000	1.5	7.9
Others	0	21,000	0	1.1

In 2011, the SNP had a disproportional number of constituency MSPs (a higher percentage of seats than their percentage of votes), while other parties had too few. This is where the additional (regional) members come into play.

AMS REGIONS

Scottish Parliament regions.

Under AMS, Scotland is also divided up into eight larger regions. Each region elects seven regional (list) MSPs.

To vote for regional MSPs, voters mark an 'X' next to their preferred party (not candidate). The parties – not voters – choose the order of the candidates on their list: the higher up the list a candidate is in their region, the more likely they are to get elected.

The regional votes for each party are used to top up the number of MSPs a party gets to give as proportional an overall result as possible. The regional list MSPs are the additional members the system is named after.

Scottish Parliament elections 2011: regional scoreboard

Party	Number of seats	Number of votes	Seats (%)	Votes (%)
Labour	22	524,000	39	26.3
SNP	16	876,000	29	44.0
Conservative	12	246,000	21	12.4
Others	3	242,000	5	12.1
Liberal Democrat	3	103,000	5	5.2

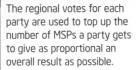

DON'T FORGET

The regional votes for each party are used to top up the number of MSPs a party gets to give as proportional an overall result as possible.

contd

As you can see in the table, in 2011 the SNP were over-represented in constituency seats. To make the result more proportional, the SNP is under-represented in regional seats.

This is designed to give an overall result that is reasonably proportional.

Scottish Parliament elections 2011: overall result

Party	Number of seats	Number of votes	Seats (%)	Votes (%)
SNP	69	1,779,336	53.5	44.7
Labour	37	1,154,020	28.7	29.0
Conservative	15	522,619	11.6	13.1
Liberal Democrat	5	399,346	3.9	10.0
Others	3	124,952	2.3	3.1

ADVANTAGES AND DISADVANTAGES OF AMS

AMS has many advantages and disadvantages. Some of these are summarised below.

Advantages	Disadvantages
Voters have more choice as they can vote for a candidate they really like (even if they're not from the party they support) and also for their preferred party.	It could be confusing for some voters who may think one of the ballots is for a 'second choice'.
Small parties have a realistic chance of being elected.	Extremist parties could get elected.
Constituency MSPs keep a strong constituency link.	People may not even know who their regional MSP is, limiting their ability to really represent their constituents.
There are few wasted votes as the regional vote allows voters to have a say even if their constituency choice loses.	Regional MSPs may be seen as second-class MSPs – elected at the second attempt.
It gives roughly proportional results.	List MSPs are more accountable to the party leadership than to their voters, so voters may not be as well represented as the numbers suggest.
AMS is likely to lead to a coalition government, giving laws based on a variety of views: 2011 was the first time Scotland had a majority government under AMS.	Coalition governments can take a long time to reach decisions and/or make decisions that nobody voted for.

VIDEO LINK
Watch 'BBC Class Clips – AMS explained' at www.brightredbooks.net/N5ModernStudies.

FACT
The 2011 Scottish election was the first time in Scotland that there had been a majority government: the previous three governments had either been a coalition or a minority government.

ONLINE TEST
Test your knowledge of AMS online at www.brightredbooks.net/N5ModernStudies.

THINGS TO DO AND THINK ABOUT

1   Use the 2011 Scottish Parliament election results to find examples of the advantages and disadvantages of the additional member system.

2   Find your constituency's result from the 2011 Scottish Parliament election using the BBC's 'Find your constituency' tool: http://www.bbc.co.uk/news/special/election2011/constituency/html/36133.stm.
    ● Find out the share of votes your constituency MSP won with.
    ● Work out the number of wasted votes in your constituency.

3   Find out your region's result from the 2011 Scottish Parliament election using the BBC's 'Find your constituency' tool: http://www.bbc.co.uk/news/special/election2011/region/html/scotland.stm.
    ● Find out which parties are represented in your region.

THE SINGLE TRANSFERABLE VOTE

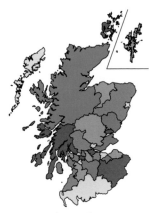

Local council areas.

City of Edinburgh Council wards.

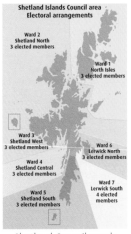

Shetland Council wards.

HOW STV WORKS

The **Single Transferable Vote** (STV) system is used to elect local councillors in Scotland. Local elections in Scotland did use FPTP, but the Liberal Democrats bargained with Labour in the 2003–2007 coalition government to have STV introduced in time for the 2007 elections.

STV is a form of proportional representation. This means that the election results should mean that the share of representatives elected for each party should quite closely reflect the share of votes for that party.

Scotland is divided up into 32 local authorities, which are responsible for making local decisions in their area (see pages 24–25). Each of these local authorities is divided up into a number of multi-member wards (like mini-constituencies). Each ward elects three or four councillors. This means that more densely populated areas (cities) have more, and geographically smaller, wards. More rural areas (the countryside) have fewer, geographically larger, wards.

HOW TO VOTE

To vote in an STV election, voters are given a sheet of paper with the names of all the candidates on it (a ballot paper). Parties are able to put forward many candidates for each ward. This is because three or four councillors are elected for each ward, and of course each party wants to have as many elected as possible!

To vote, voters number the candidates in order of preference ('1' being the first choice, '2' being next favourite, and so on).

Local Government Election Results 2012

Ward 10 – Meadows/Morningside

Candidates Elected

Name	Party	Stage Elected
Mark McInnes	Scottish Conservative and Unionist	One
Melanie Main	Scottish Green Party	Two
Paul Godzik	The Labour & Co-operative Party	Two
Sandy Howat	Scottish Nationalist Party (SNP)	Seven

Results from City of Edinburgh Council, Meadows/Morningside ward, 2012.

In order to be elected, a candidate does not need a majority of votes, just a **quota**, or share of votes. The quota required depends on the size of the electorate (number of voters) and the number of councillors to be elected in that ward. For a four-member ward, the quota is 20% of the total vote; for a three-member ward, the quota is 25% of the total vote.

In the Edinburgh ward of Meadows/Morningside, Mark McInnes won 29.9% of the first preference ('1') votes and he was therefore elected at stage 1.

EDINBURGH CITY COUNCIL: LEITH WALK WARD

Three of the candidates listed below will be elected.

You can make as many or as few choices as you wish.

Put the number 1 in the voting box next to your **first** choice.
Put the number 2 in the voting box next to your **second** choice.
Put the number 3 in the voting box next to your **third** choice. And so on.

BALFOUR, Jeremy
6 Featherhall Drive, Corstorphine
Scottish Conservative and Unionist Party

BROCK, Deirdre L
3 Lorne Avenue, Edinburgh
Scottish National Party

BUCHANAN, Tom
2 Little Lane, Liberton
Scottish National Party

BURNS, Andrew
78 Buccleugh Avenue, Edinburgh
Scottish Labour Party

CHAPMAN, Maggie
6 Bellevue Lane, Broughton
Scottish Green Party

DUNBAR, William Henry
122 Mountcastle Avenue South, Portobello
Independent

FROST, Mark
24 Leadervale Crescent, Liberton
Independent

MACLAREN, Marilyne Angela
19/10 Fowler Street, Edinburgh
Scottish Liberal Democrats

MILLIGAN, Eric
2 Craigleight Terrace, Edinburgh
Scottish Labour Party

MUNN, Rob
67 Montgomery Road
Scottish National Party

ROSE, Cameron
21 Blair Close, Edinburgh
Scottish Conservative and Unionist Party

WHITTAKER, Judith
3/3 Inverleith Court, Edinburgh
Scottish Socialist Party

Local election ballot paper.

contd

Once a candidate is elected (has met the quota), any votes they still have are called **surplus votes**. These votes are then reallocated (redistributed) to the next-preference candidates. For example, if the candidate voted '1' on a ballot already has more than the quota of votes, any surplus vote is reallocated to the candidate voted '2'. Each time votes are reallocated, this is called a stage of counting.

If there are still councillors to be elected after all the elected candidates' surplus votes have been redistributed, then the candidate with the fewest votes by that stage is eliminated, and their next-preference votes are reallocated to the other candidates.

This means that very few votes are wasted, as nearly all of them will contribute to the result at some stage.

STV has many advantages and disadvantages. Some of these are summarised below.

Party	Councils		Councillors	
	Total	+/–	Total	+/–
Scottish National Party	2	+2	424	+57
Labour	4	+2	394	+58
Conservative	0	0	115	–16
Liberal Democrat	0	0	71	–80
Green	0	0	14	+6
Scottish Socialist Party	0	0	1	0
Independent	3	0	0	0
British National Party	0	0	0	0
Independent Community and Health Concern	0	0	0	0
Liberal	0	0	0	–1
Residents Association	0	0	0	0
Respect	0	0	0	0
Socialist	0	0	0	0
UK Independence Party	0	0	0	–1
Others	0	0	201	–22
No Overall Control	23	–4		

Scottish local council election results 2012.

Advantages	Disadvantages
STV results in fewer wasted votes. There is no need for tactical voting, and voters may be more encouraged to vote when they can see that their vote counts.	Counting the votes takes a long time and many stages. It may take some time for people to know who is representing them.
STV gives voters more choice than any other voting system. Voters can choose not just a candidate from one party, but can rank-order all the candidates, from every party.	Voters may not know any candidates, never mind many from one party. In this case, it may be better to have parties put forward their best candidates for their safest seats.
As there are multi-member wards, parties are likely to try to appeal to as many voters as they can. This means they might put forward more female and ethnic minority candidates.	In large multi-member wards, with many candidates from the same party, the **ballot paper** may be big and confusing.
After the election, constituents have a choice of councillors to approach with their concerns.	To have enough voters, some wards are extremely large. Voters in remote areas of such wards may rarely see any councillors.
STV is likely to lead to a coalition local government or one under no overall control, giving laws based on a variety of views.	Coalition governments can take a long time to reach decisions and/or make decisions that nobody voted for.

VIDEO LINK

Check out 'BBC Class Clips – STV explained using ceilidh dancers' at www.brightredbooks.net/N5ModernStudies.

ONLINE TEST

Test your knowledge of STV online at www.brightredbooks.net/N5ModernStudies.

THINGS TO DO AND THINK ABOUT

1   Find out which local authority you live in and use their website to find out the results of the 2012 local elections in your ward.

   Which stage was each councillor elected in?

2   What examples can you find of the advantages and disadvantages of STV using 2012 local council elections:
   * in your ward
   * in your council
   * across the whole of Scotland?

3   Hold a class STV election!
   * Get yourselves into groups of three or four people.
   * Each group will represent a different political party: Conservative, Independent, Labour, Liberal Democrat, local issue party (make some up!), SNP, etc.
   * Copy out the ballot paper, adding the names of all the candidates.
   * Vote by numbering your candidates in order of preference: '1' being the highest, '2' next and so on.
   * Use the 'STV election results collater' (www.brightredbooks.net/N5ModernStudies) to work out the election results.

   a   What do your class results tell you about STV?

   b   How many votes were wasted?

PRESSURE GROUPS

WHY JOIN A PRESSURE GROUP?

Pressure groups are organisations of people who all believe strongly in the same cause or issue. They aim to influence governments or other decision makers. By working together, pressure groups are likely to be more successful than individual people working alone: strength in numbers.

Elections are years apart, so joining a pressure group gives the public a more regular chance to let those in power know what they think. Pressure group action can also be a much more clear and powerful statement than voting.

Many of the public are disillusioned with political parties, politicians and elections. Pressure groups give the public a different way of getting involved in politics.

TYPES OF PRESSURE GROUPS

Insider pressure groups

Confederation of British Industry

National Farmers Union (Scotland)

British Medical Association (Scotland)

There are two main types of pressure groups in Scotland and the UK. Insider pressure groups are pressure groups that work closely and formally with the government and political parties. They are usually experts in a particular area of important government policy, and so the government benefits from this group's knowledge and skills in the area. The British Medical Association (BMA) and BMA Scotland (which also act as trade unions) hold meetings with government ministers and their departments, and provide the relevant parliament with research evidence for debates and expert witnesses for committee inquiries.

Outsider pressure groups are pressure groups that do not have such privileged access to decision makers. Unlike insider pressure groups, they cannot rely on being able to have face-to-face time to persuade the government about their point of view. This makes it more difficult to influence policy, so outsider pressure groups often have to resort to more extreme measures to get their point across.

Outsider pressure groups

GREENPEACE

Animal Liberation Front

THEROBINHOODTAX

PRESSURE GROUP ACTION

There are many different types of action that pressure groups can take when they are concerned about an issue. Some of these are legal and official, others are not.

Lobbying

Pressure groups have the right to try to meet MPs and MSPs to try to convince them about the issue they are concerned with. This can be done through letter, or by actually going to parliament to try to meet the MP or MSP face to face.

Petitions

Pressure groups often use petitions to put their point across. **Petitions** are calls for action by decision makers, which the public can sign if they agree with the action they want to happen. The more people who sign them, the more likely the decision maker is to consider taking that action. These days, petitions are usually done online: e-petitions.

The Scottish Parliament Public Petitions Committee exists only to consider petitions that are submitted by concerned groups (or even individuals). They even provide a template, an online petition tool, to make it easy for people to have a say.

If an e-petition to the UK Government gets 100,000 signatures, it will be debated by the House of Commons. An MP can, however, choose to represent the views expressed in a petition by personally raising the issue in parliament.

contd

International pressure group Avaaz presented an 83,000-signature petition, started by an Afghani interpreter for the British Army, to the UK Government asking for them to grant **asylum** to all Afghani interpreters for UK soldiers. In May 2013, the UK Government did decide to offer asylum to around 600 – a notable change of mind – but Avaaz felt it was 'too limited'.

Demonstrations and protests

Demonstrations and protests allow pressure groups to gain a lot of media attention for their cause. Gaining media attention allows the general public to hear about the pressure group's cause, and also allows the government and other decision makers to see how strongly people feel about the issue. Protesting is legal, but occasionally things get out of hand and some people are arrested.

On 8 December 2012, the pressure group UK Uncut held demonstrations in Starbucks stores around the UK to demand that the UK Government changes tax rules to stop companies like the coffee chain being able to avoid paying taxes.

Direct action

When a pressure group feels that it has exhausted all other ways of effecting change, they may resort to direct action. This is where a pressure group takes the law into their own hands and changes what they feel strongly about themselves. This form of pressure group action is illegal and its members (and perhaps even leadership) can be arrested because of it.

On 16 July 2012, Greenpeace activists shut down 74 Shell petrol stations in London and Edinburgh in protest at the company's plans to drill for oil in the Arctic. There were 24 arrests: 18 in London and 6 in Edinburgh.

A much more extreme example is the frequent actions of the Animal Liberation Front. This pressure group campaigns for the freedom of animals from ownership by companies. It takes extreme and highly illegal action to reach its aims, calling for 'abolition by any means necessary'.

Pressure groups and the media

Pressure groups aim to get the public interested in an issue, and get the government to do something about it. Getting the media's attention is a key way they can do this.

First, pressure groups hope that by raising the profile of their chosen issue, they can get many more members to join the group. This will give them more resources (active members and money) to further build their campaign. They will have increased strength in numbers. If getting a campaign shown in the media convinces the public, the government and other political parties might start to support it in the hope of attracting votes at the next election.

Large campaigns may force the companies or organisations directly involved to change the way they operate, without the need for government action, in order to look good to their customers. When UK Uncut (and others) highlighted Starbucks' limited tax payments, the company volunteered to pay £20m to the government. UK Uncut described it as 'a desperate attempt to deflect public pressure'.

  UK Uncut

 GREENPEACE

Rights	Responsibilities
To recruit new members and speak on their behalf	To truly represent the views of their members
To give out or publish information flyers and posters highlighting their cause	To ensure that all information is true and that nobody has their reputation damaged through untrue accusations
To criticise the government or other decision makers	
To protest and demonstrate	To inform police beforehand, allowing police to minimise disruption to the public by re-routing traffic, for example
	To remain within the law

Rights and responsibilities of pressure groups

THINGS TO DO AND THINK ABOUT

1 Find other examples of each of the types of pressure group action listed above. You can use an internet search like 'pressure group protest 2013' to get you started.

2 Research and make notes on a campaign by any of the pressure groups shown above.

   a What is the campaign about?

   b What does it hope to change?

   c What actions has it taken?

3 'The anti-cuts demonstrations of 26 March 2012 showed the best and the worst sides of pressure group action'. (View of a journalist).

   Watch the video at http://www.guardian.co.uk/society/2011/mar/27/anti-cuts-protest-police-arrest-200 and give evidence to support this point of view.

TRADE UNIONS

WHY JOIN A TRADE UNION?

Trade unions are organisations that exist to represent workers or employees. Most employers want to cut down on costs by having workers work longer and paying as low wages as possible, while most employees would prefer more time off and higher pay for the work they do. Trade unions give workers strength in numbers in their discussions with their employers. Each workplace will have a union representative whom members can meet with if they need assistance and who will communicate with the union on their behalf. A union representative is also called a **shop steward**.

AIMS OF TRADE UNIONS

Trade unions have a number of main aims. First, they seek to represent their workers when they are unhappy at work. Second, they educate members about their rights in the workplace. They also negotiate on members' behalf when working conditions like pay are to change, providing strength in numbers.

TYPES OF TRADE UNION

There are three main types of trade union in the UK. Craft unions represent workers with a particular skill. There are very few of these in the UK now, but one example is Equity, which represents actors and models.

Industrial unions represent all workers in one industry who have different skills. An example of this is ASLEF, the Association of Locomotive Engineers and Firemen.

General unions represent workers from different industries. Unite is a general union and is the UK's biggest union.

TRADE UNION ACTION

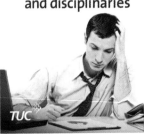

There are many ways trade unions can take action in order to fulfil their aims.

Advice

Shop stewards (union representatives) can tell the union's members about how they can and should act in any work-based situation. On a wider scale, trade unions also often publish documents, widely available online, which detail the rights workers have in certain circumstances.

Negotiation

Trade unions can represent their members within the workplace during individual disputes, usually through the shop steward having meetings with the management. If a worker feels they are being unfairly pressured to do overtime, their shop steward could discuss this with management. When many workers are to be affected by bigger changes in an industry, trade unions will try to meet with those making the decisions in order to make the outcome as beneficial to its members as possible.

When there is to be a change in Scottish teachers' pay or conditions, the Educational Institute of Scotland (EIS) sends representatives to the Scottish Negotiating Committee for Teachers (SNCT) so that teachers are represented in discussions with local councils (employers) and the Scottish Government.

contd

Lobbying

Unite is running a 'Save our Safety' campaign in the construction industry. On 11 June 2013, workers attended a mass lobby of MPs at the Houses of Parliament in London, in which they told MPs of their daily concerns about health and safety at work. This lobby took place to highlight their issue to decision makers and to the media, to try and persuade people that things need to change.

Demonstrations

Trade unions often hold **demonstrations**, where members can meet and march together to highlight concerns the unions have. These demonstrations attract a great deal of media attention and draw the wider public's attention to the issues that the unions are raising.

In October 2012, an estimated 100,000 workers from the **public sector** (those employed by the government) held demonstrations in London, Glasgow and Belfast against the UK coalition government's cuts to public sector spending.

Industrial action

If negotiation fails, trade unions can take **industrial action**. This is any action that the trade union takes to disrupt normal working patterns. It is used as a last resort to show employers how seriously workers feel about the issue. Before starting industrial action, trade unions must hold a secret ballot of their members and the majority must approve it. This is to ensure that this action will represent the members' views. There are many different forms of industrial action, some of which are detailed here.

An overtime ban is when workers refuse to work any time outside their contracted hours. This may stop the employer making as much profit as they would hope.

A work-to-rule is when a union tells it members to do exactly what their contracts tell them they have to and not anything more. The National Union of Journalists (NUJ) members at the BBC took part in a work-to-rule at BBC Scotland in January 2013, and at the BBC in the rest of the UK a month later, in protest at jobs not being redeployed to staff who were losing jobs.

A strike is when workers refuse to work. This is the most well-known and strongest form of industrial action. This is the very last resort that unions can take. On 30 November 2011, between 1 and 2 million public sector workers, including teachers, went on strike throughout the UK in protest at changes to their pensions.

Trade unions and the media

Trade unions seek to gain a great deal of media attention for their dispute. By informing the wider public through media coverage, they hope to gain wider public support. This in turn can, they hope, put pressure on their employers over the issue.

VIDEO LINK

Watch the clip 'Unite 'Save our Safety' campaign lobbies parliament' at www.brightredbooks.net/N5ModernStudies.

ONLINE

Find out more about the October 2012 anti-cuts demonstration at www.brightredbooks.net/N5ModernStudies.

VIDEO LINK

Watch the BBC film about the 30 November 2011 public sector strike and take notes on the arguments for and against this particular strike at www.brightredbooks.net/N5ModernStudies

ONLINE TEST

Take the test on trade unions online at www.brightredbooks.net/N5ModernStudies.

Rights of trade unions	Responsibilities of trade unions
To be consulted in and informed of decisions taken by the employer during a dispute.	To make sure that the shop steward is elected or chosen by the union members, and that the shop steward represents the members' true interests.
To have a shop steward (representative) in a place of work.	To represent the true interests of their members during any dispute.
To lobby local and national politicians or decision makers to try to gain their support for their cause, perhaps putting pressure on the employer about the issue.	To present the decision makers with the facts of the issue so they are fully informed before deciding whether or not to support the trade union over the issue.
To hold demonstrations to highlight their cause to the media and the public.	To not break the law during demonstrations.
	To inform police before a demonstration to allow them to plan for disruption.
To take part in industrial action: strikes, overtime bans, work-to-rules.	To hold a secret ballot of members before any industrial action is taken.
	To not force members to take part in any action.

THINGS TO DO AND THINK ABOUT

1 Research another trade union, perhaps the one that would represent you in your planned career: Find examples of this trade union representing their members in a range of ways.

THE MEDIA: TV

ROLE OF THE MEDIA

The **media** is crucial to how a democratic society works. A free press gives people the chance to learn about the decisions made by governments and parliaments. Representatives are chosen to speak up for the public; it is crucially important that the public have a chance to question them on their decisions and actions.

There are three main functions of the media in a democracy:

- to keep the public informed about what is going on
- to allow representatives' decisions to be scrutinised (looked at closely)
- to give the public a chance to express their points of view.

INFLUENCING DECISION MAKERS

In performing these roles, the media can have an important influence on the decisions made by those in power. Nearly everyone in Scotland and the UK sees or hears at least one form of media, so the message that the public receive from the media can have a big effect on the actions and popularity of the government and other parties and politicians.

FACT

TV licence costs (2013):
£145.50 (colour TV)
£49.00 (black and white TV)
Free for over-75s

TV

In the UK, TV coverage of political issues and parties must be neutral by law. This means that TV companies should allow parties a fair chance to put their point of views across and cannot show that they prefer one party over another. The BBC in particular is under strict control as the public pay for it through a licence fee.

Each of the TV stations in the UK devotes a considerable amount of time to political issues. The four terrestrial broadcasters (BBC, ITV/STV, Channel 4 and Channel 5) all have news bulletins as well as other current affairs or political shows such as Newsnight, Politics Now and Dispatches.

Boris Johnson

In each of these programmes, however, the journalists and presenters are entitled to ask difficult and probing questions that can often make life very difficult for the politician in question.

In March 2013, London Mayor Boris Johnson (Conservative) was questioned very thoroughly by BBC presenter Eddie Mair on the 'Andrew Marr Show'.

contd

When asked about the show afterwards, Johnson stated: 'He was perfectly within his rights to have a bash at me – in fact it would have been shocking if he hadn't. If a BBC presenter can't attack a nasty Tory politician, what's the world coming to?'

Party political broadcasts and party election broadcasts

Party political broadcasts (PPBs) are TV (or radio) broadcasts produced by political parties in which they put forward their point of view or criticise opposition parties. Party election broadcasts (PEBs) are broadcasts of this type that are broadcast during an election campaign. They are one of very few ways that political parties can publicise their message through the media without any journalists or editors altering or interpreting it.

TV leaders' debates

Televised leaders' debates were held for the first time in the UK for the 2010 UK general election and the 2011 Scottish Parliamentary election. The three general election debates were on ITV, Sky TV and BBC, and attracted audiences of over 9 million, around 4 million and over 8 million viewers, respectively.

Many thought that doing well in front of such large numbers of viewers would lead to success in elections. However, despite Nick Clegg's successful performances in these debates, the Liberal Democrats only managed to increase their overall share of the vote by 1% in the 2010 general election, actually winning fewer seats.

There were four Scottish debates before the 2011 election and they reached around 780,000 viewers. Many believe that Alex Salmond's confident performances helped create the SNP's victory in the election.

THINGS TO DO AND THINK ABOUT

Find TV or online coverage of a pressure group or trade union campaign. Does the coverage seem to be in favour of the action or not? Note down any parts of the report that make you think this.

VIDEO LINK

Watch the 2010 party election broadcasts for the Conservatives, Labour, Liberal Democrats and Greens, and the 2011 broadcast for the SNP at www.brightredbooks.net/N5ModernStudies.

ONLINE TEST

Take the 'Media' test online at www.brightredbooks.net/N5ModernStudies

THE MEDIA: NEWSPAPERS AND NEW MEDIA

NEWSPAPERS

Many people in Britain read a newspaper every day.

Unlike the broadcast media, TV and radio, newspapers are allowed to openly support a party. Owners and editors of newspapers hope that the way they present the parties, candidates and policies will influence the public into voting for a preferred candidate/party.

Newspaper ownership

In Britain, all the national press is owned by only seven companies, and the top four account for about 90% of sales. News International Limited, owned by Rupert Murdoch, own BSkyB (largely), *The Sun*, *The Sun on Sunday*, *The Times* and *The Sunday Times*; while the Daily Mail and General Trust plc own the *Daily Mail*, the *Mail on Sunday*, *Metro* and DMG Broadcasting (which has stakes in ITN and Reuters).

Some people argue that with so many media outlets being owned by so few people or groups, fewer and fewer different political opinions will be heard. If an important role of the media is to inform the public, this could be damaging.

Newspapers and election campaigns

In the run-up to elections, newspapers often dedicate a considerable amount of space to their preferred party or candidate.

In the UK in 2010, *The Sun* supported the Conservative Party, 13 years after changing from the Conservatives to Labour.

Before the 2011 Scottish Election, *The Scottish Sun* performed a similar U-turn, supporting the SNP running the headline: 'Play it again, Salm', after warning voters in 2007 that 'vote SNP today and you put Scotland's head in a noose'.

Some people argue that newspapers influence the voters that read them and therefore have a large influence on the outcomes of elections. Others argue that the biggest newspapers switch to whichever party is likely to win, to seem in line with public opinion. Others argue that people will buy whichever newspaper backs up their opinion and so they don't affect the results of elections.

Newspapers and political coverage

Another way that the (non-broadcast) media can influence the government is through their coverage of government decisions. While the radio and TV have to be neutral about government actions – or at least treat each party in the same way – the print media can clearly show its displeasure at government decisions. By reporting the actions of government in a positive or negative light, the media hope the government will reconsider the decisions they don't like.

Online newspaper coverage from the BBC of the cost of Margaret Thatcher's funeral.

No 10: Baroness Thatcher's funeral cost taxpayer £3.6m

Public spending on Baroness Thatcher's funeral totalled £3.6m, Downing Street has announced.

contd

In these examples, Scotland's biggest two broadsheet newspapers disagreed about whether an independent Scotland could keep its banknotes: an important question for Finance Secretary John Swinney to answer.

The Scotsman:

Coverage of Scottish bank notes question, 22 April 2013.

news.scotsman.com

Scottish independence: Banknotes safe - Swinney

The Herald:

Scottish banknotes at risk under Yes vote, warns Treasury

Monday 22 April 2013

NEW MEDIA

In previous elections people relied on the traditional media of TV, radio and newspapers. In recent elections, however, new digital media has begun to have an effect.

All parties now have Facebook groups, and nearly every MP and MSP has a Twitter account. This allows these parties and representatives to reach out to the public and journalists instantly. The public and journalists can also contact them in return.

Nearly all parties now have YouTube channels as well. This gives them a chance to broadcast their political messages over the internet to an almost infinite audience.

Mumsnet is a forum-based website where parents can speak about the issues that are important to them. Parents are, of course, a large proportion of the UK population, and it would help a politician get elected if they could win support from this group. On 3 May 2010, then Labour leader Gordon Brown held a live webchat with members after David Cameron had done the same on 19 November 2009. Alex Salmond did the same on 15 February 2011.

Rights and responsibilities of the media

Right	Responsibility
To report on what is happening in the country	To tell the truth
To investigate potential wrongdoing by public figures	To remain within the law and respect people's right to privacy (for example not to hack into people's phones)
To publish details of government spending	To not harm national security by revealing official secrets

THINGS TO DO AND THINK ABOUT

1. The media is a crucial factor in electoral success. Use examples on the past four pages to give arguments for and against this statement.

2. Try to find three different newspapers' coverage of the same political issue.

   Compare the ways these are covered. Are they in favour or against? How can you tell?

3. Have a look at the Facebook page or Twitter feed of one of the main political parties.

   What sort of comments and tweets do they post?

 FACT

11% of people were contacted through social media by political parties in the run-up to the 2010 UK general election.

SOURCE-BASED QUESTIONS: AN OVERVIEW

These questions are worth 8 marks in the final exam.

You will be given between two and four sources containing a range of information. Some of these will contain written information, while others will contain numbers, in graphs or charts.

Also, you will be given a sentence or two that someone has said: the 'quote', 'view' or 'statement'.

Source 1: Selected female political representation in the UK 2000–2013

	2000	2004	2008	2013	Net change 2000/2013
Members of Parliament (MPs)	18.4%	18.1%	19.3%	22.5%	+4.1%
The Cabinet	21.7%	27.3%	26.1%	17.4%	−3.5%
Members of the Scottish Parliament (MSPs)	37.2%	39.5%	34.1%	35.7%	−1.5%
Local councillors	29.0%	30.0%	30.0%	32.0%	+3.0%
UK Members of the European Parliament (MEPs)	23.9%	24.4%	25.6%	33.3%	+9.4%

From *Sex and Power Report 2013*

Source 2: Women in politics

The late Baroness Thatcher was a very important and famous figure in British politics. She was elected as an MP in 1959 and became Conservative Party leader in 1975. She served as Britain's first and so far only female Prime Minister for 11 years from 1979 to 1990, winning three general election victories. She entered the House of Lords in 1992, and served until her death in April 2013.

Diane Abbott MP was elected to the UK Parliament in 1987, the first black woman to gain this position. She was appointed Shadow Minister for Public Health in 2010. Prime Minister David Cameron has pledged to make a third of his Cabinet female by 2015.

In the Labour Party leadership contest of 2010, Diane Abbott was the only woman to run, and she finished last in the ballot. The Green Party is currently the only UK party led by a woman.

In the Scottish Parliament, three out of the five parties are led by men. Johann Lamont is the leader of the Scottish Labour Party. First elected in 1999, and in every Scottish Parliament election since, she was elected leader in December 2011. Ruth Davidson MSP is leader of the Scottish Conservatives. She was elected to the Scottish Parliament in May 2011 and became leader in November of the same year.

The UK is currently ranked joint 58th in the world for female representation in a national parliament. The world leader is Rwanda, with 56%. At the current rate of progress, it will take 200 years – another 40 elections – to achieve an equal number of women in parliament in the UK.

Four of the last five leaders of the House of Lords have been women, and 41% of appointments made by the House of Lords Appointments Commission since 2004 have been women.

In the 2012 Scottish local council elections, one in four candidates was a woman. In one in seven council elections, there were only male candidates standing for election.

Source 3: Women as a percentage of MPs for each political party in 2000 and 2012

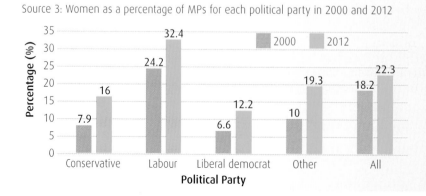

contd

Source 4: Claims of sexism in UK politics

In April 2011, David Cameron drew criticism for telling a female MP to 'calm down dear' during a Commons debate.

Former Conservative MP Louise Mensch demanded an apology from Labour MP Austin Mitchell in October 2012 after he tweeted to tell her 'a good wife doesn't disagree with her master in public', after her husband seemed to suggest a different reason for her leaving parliament.

Similarly, in January 2013, Murdo Fraser, MSP for Mid-Scotland and Fife, found out that the wife of former Liberal leader Lord Steel had said she was in favour of Scottish independence. He tweeted: 'Why is Lady Steel (apparently) pro-independence? Is he not master in his own house?'

In March 2013, Liberal Democrat youth leader Kav Kaushik said she may leave, and tweeted 'the sexism is too much for me now'.

In a speech in May 2013, Diane Abbott MP said that some parts of British culture see sexism and homophobia as normal, and expressed concern at the impression this was having on young men in the UK.

EXAGGERATION

VIDEO LINK

Head to the BrightRED Digital Zone and watch the clip 'Are these examples of political spin?' to see debate about potential moments of political spin and how exaggeration is used in parliament.

In these questions, you are given a quote/view and have to find part of the quote that is not accurate. This might be a whole sentence or part of a sentence.

You have to then describe the evidence that proves the quote is incorrect. Each reason you give can get up to 3 marks, depending on how accurately you use your sources and how well you develop your argument.

Just writing down a piece of evidence from a source will only get 1 mark.

Answering an 'exaggeration' question

Using sources 1, 2, 3 and 4 above, explain why Gavin Johnson is exaggerating.

'Fewer women are being elected in politics, and women who are elected only take on minor roles in their party. Sexism is a problem only within the Labour Party.'

View of Gavin Johnson

- You should give information that shows Gavin Johnson is exaggerating.

Your answer must be based on all four sources.   **8 marks**

A 3-mark section of an answer to this question could look like this:

The quote which is exaggerated.	*Gavin Johnson could be accused of exaggeration when he says 'Fewer women are being elected*
Evaluative terminology	*in politics'. The evidence* **clearly** *shows that* **the percentage of women being elected to the UK**
Evidence from the sources which proves the exaggeration	**Parliament increased** *considerably* **between 2000 and 2013, from 18.4% to 22.5%** *(Source 1).*
The sources of the information	*Source 3 backs this up by showing that* **the percentage of female Conservative MPs increased** *hugely* **from 7.9% to 16%. These figures show**
Developed discussion of the evidence	**that the number of women being elected has got much larger** *in the past few elections.*

ONLINE TEST

Take the 'Source-based questions' test online at www.brightredbooks.net/N5ModernStudies.

To get full marks, this answer would need to have two more sections, one at least this good and one that wasn't quite as full an answer (2 marks).

THINGS TO DO AND THINK ABOUT

Complete the 'exaggeration' question above to get the rest of the 8 marks.

SOURCE-BASED QUESTIONS: SELECTIVE IN THE USE OF FACTS

DON'T FORGET

The way to get really good marks is to use information from different sources – *synthesis* – to make each point, and develop your argument using **evaluative terminology**.

SELECTIVE IN THE USE OF FACTS

In source-based questions you are given a quote/view and have to describe ways in which the evidence supports the quote (shows it may be true) *and* ways in which the evidence does not support the quote (shows it may be untrue).

If you only discuss evidence on one side (supporting or opposing the quote), you can only get 6 marks.

Each reason you give can get up to 3 marks, depending on how accurately you use your sources and how well you develop your argument.

Answering a 'Selective in the use of facts' question

> Using Sources 1, 2, 3 and 4 above [see pages 44–45], explain why the view of Kevin Coutts is selective in the use of the facts.
>
> > 'The UK political system is moving towards gender equality.'
> >
> > View of Kevin Coutts
>
> In your answer you must:
>
> - give evidence from the sources that supports Kevin Coutts's view; and
> - give evidence from the sources that oppose Kevin Coutts's view.
>
>   Your answer must be based on all four sources. **8 marks**

A 3-mark section of an answer to this question could look like this:

The quote that is exaggerated	*Kevin Coutts is being selective when he says 'The UK political system is moving towards gender equality' as the proportion of women in positions of power is* **clearly decreasing** *in many cases.* **The share of women in the UK Cabinet decreased from 21.7% to 17.4% between 2000 and 2013:** *a significant 3.5% net decrease (Source 1).* **Although** *David Cameron has pledged to increase this number to a third before the 2015 general election (Source 2),* **he has already been accused of sexism** *in a parliamentary debate,* **telling a female Labour MP to 'calm down dear' (Source 4),** *so it may be* **very unlikely** *that he will stick to this policy of treating women fairly.*
Evaluative terminology	
Evidence from the sources which proves the exaggeration	
The sources of the information	
Developed discussion of the evidence	

To get full marks, this answer would need to have three or more sections:

- at least one other section using evidence that does not support his point of view
- at least one section using evidence that does support his point of view.

contd

DON'T FORGET

For 'selective in the use of facts' questions, you have to describe evidence that agrees with the point of view and evidence that does not agree. Only giving one side can only get you 6 marks out of 8.

When arguing source-based questions, using fewer sections that use more sources and describe the argument in more detail may earn you more marks than a number of short sections with little development of the evidence.

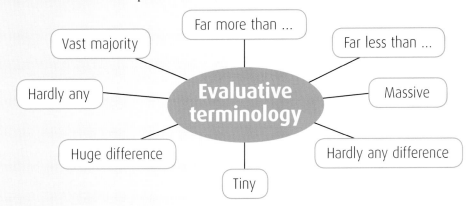

Vast majority

Far more than ...

Far less than ...

Hardly any

Evaluative terminology

Massive

Huge difference

Hardly any difference

Tiny

THINGS TO DO AND THINK ABOUT

Complete the 'selective in the use of facts' question above to get the rest of the 8 marks.

WHAT IS POVERTY?

People who live in **poverty** are considered to be those who struggle to pay for things they need. In the UK official poverty levels are measured by the Department of Work and Pensions using their Households Below the Average Income (HBAI) annual report, the latest figures for which were released in June 2013.

ABSOLUTE POVERTY

Globally, this term refers to those in less developed countries who may live on less than $1 per day and are deprived of basic human needs such as food, water, sanitation, health, shelter, education and access to support. In the UK absolute poverty is defined as anyone living on less than half the average UK annual income. In 2013 the average annual UK household income was measured at £16,034, so the absolute poverty level is £8017.

The **United Nations** (UN) defines absolute poverty as 'a condition characterised by severe deprivation of basic human needs'.

RELATIVE POVERTY

Relative poverty is socially defined according to the society in which people live, e.g. those that are worse off than the majority of others where they are. A minimum standard, known as a poverty line, is set and anyone living below that amount is considered to be living in poverty. The poverty line is usually set at 60% of the median income (middle income in a range of all UK incomes).

SOCIAL EXCLUSION

Social exclusion refers to those in poverty who are disconnected and are unable to participate in 'normal' society. People who are socially excluded cannot purchase goods or services that the average person would be able to buy, which has a severe impact on their quality of life.

GROUPS AT RISK OF POVERTY AND SOCIAL EXCLUSION

There are certain groups in society that are more at risk of poverty and social exclusion than others. The reasons for this are discussed later in this chapter.

Children and young people

Children are considered dependants, meaning that they cannot generate their own income and are reliant on adults such as their parents. Unfortunately, many children find themselves born into households in poverty and suffer as a consequence. Young people find it increasingly difficult to generate their own income, especially if they leave school at a young age with few academic qualifications.

- A boy born in one of the most deprived areas of the UK has a life expectancy of 68, which is 8 years below the national average and 14 years below that of boys born in the least deprived areas.

- Approximately 36,367 children in the Glasgow City Council area are living below the relative poverty line.

- Since 2008, the number of under-25s who are unemployed in Scotland has almost doubled to 90,000.

contd

Working age adults

Working age adults are those people who are between age 16 and their retirement age. The age people can retire varies depending on when they were born.

This group may find themselves living in poverty due to unemployment or low pay:

- The number of people working part-time and who wanted a full-time job rose from 70,000 in 2008 to 120,000 in 2012.
- As of April 2013 the UK unemployment percentage for working age adults was 7.8.

The elderly

Most people decide to stop working and retire when they reach a certain age. The UK Government currently provides a **state pension** for many of those elderly people. The current maximum amount paid to any one person is £110.15 per week (this slightly increases every year with the cost of living) and people are encouraged to take out supplementary private or **occupational pensions** throughout their working lives to top this state amount up when they retire. For some that extra saving is limited or impossible. This means there are many elderly people who are totally reliant on the state pension as their sole income when they retire and may find themselves struggling to pay for necessities and bills.

- 1.2 million pensioners are on the brink of poverty.
- Women, those aged 80 to 84, those living alone, and Pakistani and Bangladeshi people are at greater risk of pensioner poverty than other social groups.

Summary table: the number of people living in UK households with below 60% of the average UK contemporary income (after housing costs are deducted):

	2011–2012 (millions)	Percentage change since 2010–2011	Percentage change since 1998–1999
Children	3.5	0	−7
Working age adults	7.9	0	+2
Pensioners	1.6	−1	−15

(Source: *HBAI Report 2013*)

THINGS TO DO AND THINK ABOUT

1   The UK Government spends time and money gathering information on current poverty levels. Give at least two reasons why the UK Government needs this information.

2   Why can the majority of people living in poverty in the UK be described as living in relative, and not absolute, poverty?

3   According to the Office for National Statistics the average household spent £483.60 per week in 2011 (after mortgage costs).

    A family in poverty has approximately 60% of that total amount to spend per week, reducing it to £290.16.

    - Working with a partner, use the figures above to decide where a family in poverty could reduce their spending to be within their budget but still have what their family needs.

4   The age people can receive their state pension in the UK varies depending on when they were born, e.g. if they were born in 1956 they may receive a state pension in 2022 when they are 66, but if they were born in 1979, they are not due to receive their state pension until age 68.

    - Why do you think this is?

5   Answer this question using the table of 2013 HBAI statistics.

    'The UK Government is successfully tackling child poverty.'

    - Give one reason to support and one reason to oppose this statement.

ONLINE

Learn more by clicking the PSE link at www. brightredbooks.net/ N5ModernStudies.

ONLINE TEST

Revise this topic online by clicking on the 'What is poverty?' test online at www.brightredbooks.net/ N5ModernStudies.

VIDEO LINK

Check out the 'What is poverty?' clip at www. brightredbooks.net/ N5ModernStudies.

DON'T FORGET

UK unemployment statistics only measure people who are actively seeking employment.

FACT

Scottish Government statistics show that 710,000 people in Scotland, including 150,000 children, were living in relative poverty in 2011–12.

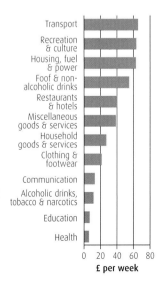

CAUSES OF POVERTY

The UK is the world's sixth-largest economy, yet one fifth of the UK population live below its official **poverty line**, meaning that they experience life as a daily struggle.

There are many reasons for this and some groups of people are more likely to live in poverty than others.

UNEMPLOYMENT/WORKLESSNESS

Most people rely on employment as a source of income. As of April 2013, the Scottish unemployment rate was 7.4%, with the UK figure at 7.8%. This figure has reduced since 2012 but is still significant.

Without a regular decent income people can find themselves living in poverty and struggling to pay bills and for the things they need.

However, some people cannot work because of health reasons, childcare issues or responsibilities such as being a carer for someone else. This is known as worklessness as they are not necessarily actively seeking employment.

Where people live may also affect their job prospects as some areas of the UK suffer from chronic unemployment and people get caught in a poverty cycle or the benefit trap, where working actually leaves people worse off. Statistics have shown a north/south divide in the UK, with unemployment and inequality higher in the north than in the south.

ONLINE

Have a look at the 'Unemployment trends' link at www.brightredbooks.net/N5ModernStudies.

ONLINE

Check out the 'Unemployment tracker' link at www.brightredbooks.net/N5ModernStudies.

VIDEO LINK

Check out the clip 'Poverty in our society' at www.brightredbooks.net/N5ModernStudies.

LOW PAY

Some jobs do not require specific training, skills or educational qualifications and as a result the pay may be very low. For example, the specific qualifications and training required to be the director of a major organisation mean directors can earn over £100,000 annually while a cleaner may earn less than £7000. This pay gap is on the basis of supply and demand. Those who have the skills most in demand are low in supply, meaning they can command higher wages than others.

Many employers now only offer part-time contracts for employees instead of full-time, significantly reducing the number of hours people can work and subsequently their pay. Those with childcare commitments have to face rising childcare costs reducing their income further. Despite the introduction of a **National Minimum Wage** (discussed later in this chapter) in 1998 many people in the UK still find themselves earning very low amounts, especially in comparison to those in roles that require very specific qualifications and training.

Low wages, part-time work and the high costs of childcare can result in low incomes.

Many low-wage jobs offer no chance of promotion ('low pay, low prospects'); others are insecure, providing only temporary and unpredictable incomes ('low pay, no pay'). As a result, they are often nothing more than poverty traps.

There are 1.4 million part-time workers wanting full-time work in the UK and 6.4 million people now lack the paid work they want.

BENEFITS SYSTEM

If a person is unemployed in the UK they may be reliant on **benefits** provided by the UK Government. However, benefits are deliberately set at low levels, leaving recipients living below the poverty line, and some of them are **means-tested**, meaning that the amounts paid can vary from person to person.

Some people may find themselves caught in the **benefit trap**, where it does not make financial sense to get a low-paid job as they will stop receiving essential benefits and may introduce new costs such as travel expenses and childcare.

The UK Government plans to limit the total annual amount households can receive from 2013 onwards to encourage people caught in this cycle back to work.

GENDER AND RACE

Inequalities in gender and race are discussed in detail later in this chapter but it is important to address the fact that women and ethnic minorities have comparatively high poverty statistics.

Gender

Despite progress in this area women are still paid less than men (up to 15%), are less likely to work at all compared to men and can suffer from discrimination in the workplace. Some employers will view a male candidate for a job or promotion as less of a risk than a female as males are less likely to have family commitments and won't require lengthy maternity leave. This is known as the **glass ceiling effect** or gender stereotyping, where women can struggle for recognition and promotion.

Many women also find themselves in caring roles, limiting the hours and types of jobs they can do. This has an impact on their income, and many women will go without basic necessities to provide for others such as their children. Women are also more likely than men to be lone parents.

Race

The poverty rate for ethnic minorities is approximately 40% compared to 20% for whites in the UK. Many minority ethnic groups suffer discrimination in the workplace and may be overlooked for jobs and promotion.

Bangladeshis and Pakistanis statistically are more at risk of poverty than other ethnic groups.

FAMILY STRUCTURE

In 2011 22% of households were headed by a lone parent. A lone-parent household may mean one income compared to a two-parent household with two. Lone parents are also less likely to work full-time or at all due to childcare restrictions, and may be totally reliant on state benefits for their income.

ONLINE TEST

Revise this topic online by clicking on the 'Causes of poverty' test online at www.brightredbooks.net/N5ModernStudies.

DON'T FORGET

There are always exceptions, e.g. not all lone-parent families live in poverty.

FACT

6.1 million people in poverty are in working households. In-work poverty figures are now higher than workless poverty, at 5.1 million households.

THINGS TO DO AND THINK ABOUT

1. Explain the difference between unemployment and worklessness.

2. Create a spider diagram of the main causes of poverty with brief summaries for each.

3. Why might some people consider themselves 'better off' receiving benefits from the UK Government than getting a low-paid job?

CONSEQUENCES OF POVERTY

ILL-HEALTH

Ill-health can affect those suffering from poverty both physically and mentally.

Depression

Thirty-one per cent of people in poverty reported having depression, while just 15.8% of people not in poverty reported having the condition. Depression is marked by dark moods, tiredness, thinking problems and trouble sleeping. Financial worries will have an effect on a person's mental state and how they will cope. Divorce is also more common in poverty, adding to the strain and onset of depression.

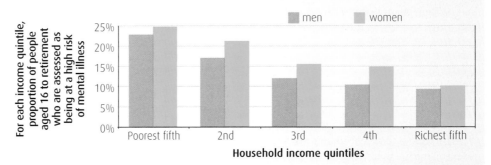

Adults in the poorest fifth of the population are much more likely to be at risk of developing a mental illness than those on average incomes.
Source: Health Survey for England, DH. Data are the average for 2008 and 2009, England, updated March 2011.

Asthma linked to poor housing

Children living in poor housing are almost twice as likely to suffer from poor health as other children. Low temperatures lower resistance to respiratory infections such as asthma. Damp in houses as a result of lack of heating leads to mould growth, which can also cause allergies. The most common cause of asthma in children is the house dust mite.

Asthma can be a terrifying experience for children. For some it can be a matter of life and death. But it's not only the physical problems of the illness that affect children. The illness will lead to increased absence from school and could have an impact on educational attainment.

Obesity and lack of exercise

Many stereotype the USA as a nation of obesity but new figures show that Scotland is fast becoming the fattest country in Europe, nearly matching American levels! A diet of junk food and inactivity means that one in eight Scottish children is officially classified as being overweight. This is predicted to worsen, with adult obesity levels reaching 40% by 2030.

This table shows the distribution of obesity from the least to most deprived households in the UK:

	Least deprived	Second	Third	Fourth	Most deprived
Obese men (%)	22	23	24	24	25
Obese women (%)	19	25	28	28	30

This would lead people to believe that calorie intake must be higher in the most deprived groups, but a recent NHS study has disputed this. It found that the poorest 10% of UK households consume on average 1845 calories per day and the richest 10% of households consume 2009 calories. Food choices vary but the impact of no exercise seems to be key. Those in poverty are less likely to take exercise, which may be due to illness or financial strain, e.g. gym memberships are expensive.

EDUCATION

It has long been suggested that education is a way out of poverty, but those in poverty have difficulty gaining an equal education. Reasons can be linked to less time being spent at home going over homework, less money invested in study books and school trips, bullying and poorer diet. The differences are obvious very early in a child's education. Only 73% of 5- to 6-year-olds from the most deprived areas in the UK achieved the expected level of writing compared to 90% of those in the least deprived (wealthiest) areas.

HOMELESSNESS

Anyone can become homeless and many homeless people have previously had successful lives. Reasons for homelessness vary between males and females. The most common reasons for males are relationship breakdown, substance misuse and leaving an institution (prison, care, hospital etc.). For homeless women, the most common causes are physical or mental health problems and escaping a violent relationship. Poverty is a common theme amongst the various reasons given.

A common assumption is that to be homeless you live on the streets; this is definitely not the case. Being homeless also takes into account:
- people living in overcrowded conditions
- those at risk of violence or abuse in their home
- living in poor conditions that affect health
- staying in temporary accommodation such as a hostel.

DON'T FORGET

Although those in poverty are *more likely* to suffer these issues it doesn't mean that everyone in poverty actually will! Try and avoid stereotyping.

ADDICTION PROBLEMS

Smoking

Smoking is strongly linked to a stressful lifestyle and many use it as a coping mechanism. Around 15% of men and 14% of women smoke cigarettes in the upper and middle classes. This number trebles for working-class males to 45% and doubles to 33% for working-class women. In the most deprived groups, such as the homeless, smoking reaches 70%. Smoking 20 cigarettes a day costs nearly £2000 per year. Those on a low income will be spending much of their disposable income on cigarettes and may be neglecting other important essentials such as heating and food, which will then have an impact on their health. The list of smoking-related illnesses includes emphysema, bronchitis, coronary artery disease, liver cancer, prostate cancer, erectile dysfunction in men, stomach cancer, bladder and kidney cancer, cataracts and cervical cancer. Those in poverty will be more likely to suffer from these diseases as a result of smoking.

'Smoking is the principal cause of the inequalities in death rates between rich and poor. Put simply, smoking is a public health disaster.'

Alan Milburn, former Secretary of State for Health

ONLINE

For more information about how smoking affects your health, visit www.brightredbooks.net/N5ModernStudies.

Drugs and alcohol

Research suggests that there is a strong association between poverty and problematic drug use. Those who are unemployed, particularly the long-term unemployed, and early school leavers have a higher rate of substance abuse. According to a 2009 UN report, Scotland is ranked second out of 47 European countries for heroin and cannabis use. The worst figures were recorded in the most socially deprived areas.

Alcohol is another form of escapism and its consumption has doubled in the UK over the last 50 years. According to the NHS it kills at least 40 Scots a week. The Scottish Government has introduced the Alcohol Minimum Pricing Bill to try and reduce alcohol consumption. Nicola Sturgeon, the former Scottish Health Secretary, believes that 'tackling alcohol misuse is one of the most important public health challenges that we face in Scotland'.

ONLINE TEST

Check your knowledge of the consequences of poverty in the UK online at www.brightredbooks.net/N5ModernStudies.

THINGS TO DO AND THINK ABOUT

Look for advantages and disadvantages of the Alcohol Minimum Pricing Bill and consider the merits of the EU and industry challenges to its passage.

TACKLING POVERTY

There are many groups and organisations that work to try to reduce poverty in the UK.

UK GOVERNMENT

The welfare state

In 1942 the Beveridge Report was published highlighting the 'five giants standing in the way of social progress'. These five giants were *want, squalor, ignorance, disease* and *idleness*, and the report specifically focused on *want*, which today we refer to as poverty. The writer of the report, William Beveridge, believed that it was the government's responsibility to tackle these 'giants' and that a **welfare state** should be introduced to do so. The founding principles of the welfare state were that it should be collectivist (state funded), universal (free at the point of need), comprehensive (available for everyone) and equal (services provided to the same standard regardless of region). This 'from the cradle to the grave' Labour government welfare state provided a National Health Service, housing, education and employment programmes, and benefits all paid for via taxation and National Insurance in order to tackle poverty and its consequences.

The Big Society and Welfare to Work

The welfare state has changed since its implementation. People are living longer and the strain on the services provided by the UK Government has meant change was inevitable. The Big Society was the idea of Prime Minister David Cameron. He believes in a more individualist approach to the welfare state and has made it clear that he wants to replace some of the responsibilities of the government with increased control of more localised organisations and private companies. This has meant significant reform to the NHS and benefits system, and aims to reduce welfare dependency.

UK legislation

Child Poverty Act 2010: The UK has set and aims to meet targets by 2020. The government will work alongside local authorities to assess specific needs and create strategies to meet them, but based on current statistics and the state of the UK economy it looks unlikely this target will be met.

Equality Act 2010: This law makes it illegal for anyone to be discriminated against on the basis of among others gender, race, age, disability or sexuality, especially in employment.

Welfare Reform Act 2012: This law aims to make the benefit system fairer and more affordable to help reduce poverty, worklessness and welfare dependency, and to reduce levels of fraud and error.

Department for Work and Pensions

The Department for Work and Pensions is responsible for administering the Welfare to Work reforms on benefits and pensions in the UK. The type and amount of benefits people receive is regularly checked and in 2013 significant changes will come into effect.

There are many benefits that people can receive in order to tackle poverty. Many of them are means tested, meaning the amount can vary per person.

Job seeker's allowance	Temporary payment paid to those actively seeking employment
Income support	Top-up payment for those on a low income
Child benefit	Paid to parents earning less than £50,000 per year for each child they have Current child benefit rates are £20.30 per week for the eldest or only child and £13.40 for each additional child

VIDEO LINK

Check out the video 'David Cameron launches the Big Society fund' at www.brightredbooks.net/ModernStudies.

ONLINE

Read more by following the 'Big Society' link at www.brightredbooks.net/ModernStudies.

FACT

In April 2011, the UK Government introduced the pupil premium. This gives schools extra funding to close attainment gaps for disadvantaged pupils. Due to devolution, this does not apply in Scotland.

ONLINE

Learn more by visiting the UK Government website at www.brightredbooks.net/ModernStudies.

Disability living allowance, employment and support allowance, personal independence payment (as of 2013)	Paid to those who cannot work due to a disability or long-term illness Claimants are individually assessed
Working tax credits	Paid to those on a low income based on their hours of work per week
Child tax credits	Paid to those on a low income who have children
Housing benefit	Payment towards housing costs for those on low or no incomes

As of October 2013, these individual benefits are gradually being replaced with one universal credit payment that is paid directly to the recipient each month like a salary, if they qualify.

In 2013 a **benefit cap** was introduced, limiting the total amount of money a household can receive in state benefits per week to:

- £500 for couples
- £500 for single parents
- £350 for single adults.

There will be some exceptions to this limit but these caps are intended to remove the benefits trap problem, where some people find themselves better off not working and claiming benefits.

Recently there have also been changes to entitlements for maternity and paternity pay, other benefits such as winter fuel and cold weather payments, grants towards improved heating and insulation, and maternity costs.

Benefit fraud and tax avoidance

Unfortunately there are people who claim benefits they are not entitled to and this is known as **benefit fraud**. The UK Government has reported that this costs £1.2 billion per year and is one of the reasons the benefit system will see so many changes.

Tax avoidance is when people don't pay the tax amount they should based on their earnings. This is legal but considered morally wrong as the people who do it tend to be very rich already! This costs the UK billions in tax each year and means less money can be spent on schemes like the welfare state. Many celebrities have recently been accused of tax avoidance.

National minimum wage

The national minimum wage was introduced to tackle income inequality and remove poverty pay, but the rates remain low and some employers struggle to pay it.

Group	2012 rate	October 2013 rate
21 and over	£6.19	£6.31
18–20	£4.98	£5.03
16–17	£3.68	£3.72
Apprentices (under 19 in their first year)	£2.65	£2.68

THINGS TO DO AND THINK ABOUT

1 Explain the difference between the collectivist and individualist approach to the welfare state

2 Create a table highlighting the arguments for and against the national minimum wage.

3 Why has it been necessary for the welfare state to change so dramatically?

ONLINE TEST

Check your knowledge of tackling poverty at www.brightredbooks.net/ N5ModernStudies.

TACKLING POVERTY AND HEALTH INEQUALITIES

VIDEO LINK

Learn more about the Child Poverty Action Group at www.brightredbooks.net/N5ModernStudies.

FACT

The Trussell Trust food bank is one of 185 food banks across the UK that can provide up to 3 days of emergency food for families in poverty.

DON'T FORGET

Social security and pensions are reserved matters currently under the control of the UK Government but the Scottish Government has the power to introduce legislation and set targets to tackle poverty and focus on groups at risk, e.g. The Housing (Scotland) Act 2001 set the target of eradicating fuel poverty in Scotland by 2016.

FACT

The Scottish Government is currently debating the Children and Young People (Scotland) Bill, which was introduced in 2013 and focuses on improving the rights and opportunities for children and young people in Scotland.

VIDEO LINK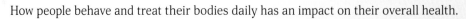

Check out the 'Health inequalities' clip at www.brightredbooks.net/N5ModernStudies.

SCOTTISH GOVERNMENT AND LOCAL AUTHORITIES

Scottish Enterprise

Scottish Enterprise (www.scottish-enterprise.com) work with businesses across Scotland to stimulate economic growth and improve the business environment. They support businesses looking to expand and create jobs by offering loans, grants and expertise.

Scottish Development International

Scottish Development International works with the Scottish Government, Scottish Enterprise and Highlands and Islands Enterprise to bring together resources and deliver support for companies, such as Samsung Heavy Industries, who are looking to invest and create jobs in Scotland.

Local authorities

The Child Poverty Act 2010 puts a duty on all local authorities to cooperate with central government and with each other to tackle child poverty. They are required to assess the needs of their local areas and create strategies to tackle specific problems.

Local authorities also provide free part-time nursery places for 3-year-olds to encourage parents back into employment, and Sure Start programmes provide support and training.

VOLUNTARY SECTOR

Local volunteers often work together to set up projects in their communities to tackle poverty and its consequences. They also lobby politicians for change.

Church Action on Poverty: Manchester (Community Pride Programme), Cranhill Community Project in the east end of Glasgow, Save the Children, Barnardo's and Oxfam are all voluntary organisations that work across the UK to tackle poverty.

The Child Poverty Action Group lobby and campaign for better lives for low-income families.

PRIVATE SECTOR

The Scottish Government works alongside private businesses and a range of agencies to tackle Scotland's youth unemployment problem as part of the More Choices, More Chances initiative.

Renewable energy company Absolute Solar and Wind has been working with sheltered housing providers in Cumbernauld to install 96 solar panel systems on sheltered housing developments. This will help to reduce their energy bills and tackle **fuel poverty**.

LIFESTYLE

How people behave and treat their bodies daily has an impact on their overall health.

Smoking, alcohol and drugs

There is a clear link between smoking and health issues such as lung cancer. Drinking alcohol excessively can significantly damage your liver and abusing drugs can result in a number of health problems and addiction.

contd

Poor diet and obesity

What people eat or don't eat has a direct impact on their health. Eating large quantities of fatty and sugary food will not only result in weight gain and obesity but also has negative health implications, such as increasing the risk of heart disease.

Recent figures show that two-thirds of adults and a third of children in Scotland are now overweight, with the cost of obesity to society rising to more than £457 million a year.

Dr Andrew Fraser of the Royal College of Physicians in Edinburgh states: 'Obesity is a direct cause of a range of life-limiting and life-reducing illnesses, including a range of cancers, heart disease and diabetes. It means people cannot work, and is also a cause of very significant financial cost to a resource-limited NHS.'

Lack of exercise

Two-thirds of men and women are not doing enough physical activity to benefit their health. In Scotland around 2500 people per year die prematurely as a result of physical inactivity, according to government statistics.

GEOGRAPHY

Statistics have shown that Scots are unhealthier than other British people. They are more likely to suffer long-term illness, take less exercise, be overweight and spend more on cigarettes and alcohol. There is a clear north/south divide when it comes to the health of Britain, with Scotland and the north of England having higher death rates than the rest of the country. Scotland also has a higher rate of lung cancer.

Life expectancy figures 2011

Area	Male	Female
Scotland	76	80
England	78.7	82.6
UK	78.5	82.5

According to 2011 statistics Glasgow had the lowest life expectancy in Scotland for men and women, while men in the Borders and women on Orkney were expected to live longest.

Three Cities Report 2013

This research, carried out by the Glasgow Centre for Population Health (GCPH), examined and compared the health and wellbeing of Glasgow, Liverpool and Manchester. The study aimed to explain Glasgow's reasons for 'excess' mortality (30% higher than the other cities) and the findings were published in June 2013.

ONLINE

Read more by following the GCPH link at www.brightredbooks.net/N5ModernStudies.

THINGS TO DO AND THINK ABOUT

1   Why might some families view the current child benefit means testing as unfair?

2   Using the internet and local media, research local projects in your area that tackle poverty. Create a leaflet/presentation to outline one of the projects, how it works and what it does.

3   Examine the life expectancy table.

   a   What conclusion can be drawn about the area with the lowest life expectancy?

   b   Why do you think this is?

ONLINE TEST

Test your knowledge of tackling poverty health inequalities at www.brightredbooks.net/N5ModernStudies.

TACKLING HEALTH INEQUALITIES 1

SOCIO-ECONOMIC DISADVANTAGES

Poverty affects where people live and their lifestyles. If you live in a run-down deprived community you're unlikely to go for a jog around your local area. Gym memberships can be expensive so people in deprived communities may not use health facilities even if they are nearby.

People on low incomes may be reliant on public transport, meaning they can't always travel to larger supermarkets and become reliant on the goods they can get from local shops, which aren't always fresh and healthy. Levels of obesity are often higher within poorer communities as a result.

People in deprived communities are more likely to suffer from depression and mental health problems. As a consequence they are more likely to smoke, drink alcohol excessively or take drugs as a release from their socio-economic disadvantages.

Sir Harry Burns, Chief Medical Officer for Scotland, has named this the 'biology of poverty'. He claims that a child born into the stress of poverty is negatively affected biologically and is more likely to succumb to ill-health than a child born elsewhere.

Social class

Social class is the category that people fall into based on their income and occupation. The lower down the social class scale you are the more likely you are to be living in poverty, and several government reports have highlighted the link between poverty and poor health. The World Health Organisation (WHO) published their findings of a 3-year health study in 2008, highlighting the effects of poverty on life expectancy. The report concluded by stating that 'social injustice is killing people on a grand scale'. For example, life expectancy can differ depending on the area you live in.

Men born in Glasgow's deprived east end will die 9 years before men born in India. And male children born a 15-minute drive away in affluent Lenzie can expect to live 28 years longer.

A World Health Organisation report out yesterday revealed life expectancy for a male child born in Calton, Glasgow, was just 54. In India, the figure is 63 and men born in Lenzie will live an average of 82 years.

(Source: Lachlan MacKinnon, *Men in Glasgow's east end have life expectancy of 54*, the *Daily Record* 29th August 2008)

ENVIRONMENT

The environment that people live in can have an impact on overall health. This can be related to pollution in built-up cities or simply the household environment or family structure a person lives in. Unhealthy or abusive parents are more likely to have unhealthy children.

AGE

As people get older their health tends to deteriorate and they may require more healthcare and support. Conditions such as osteoporosis and diseases such as Alzheimer's are more common among the elderly.

GENDER

As you can see from the life expectancy table, statistically women live longer than men in the UK but they suffer more health problems throughout their lives.

The biggest killer of Scottish women is lung cancer and women have higher death rates from conditions as a result of ageing and mental health problems than men. Surveys have shown, however, that women are more likely to seek medical advice than men.

RACE

Ethnic minorities suffer from fewer diseases related to the overconsumption of alcohol and often have healthy diets compared to the overall population. This is directly related to cultural and religious beliefs, but ethnic minorities are more likely to live in poverty than whites and suffer overall poorer health as a result.

THE SCOTTISH PARLIAMENT

As health and law and order are devolved matters, the Scottish Parliament has responsibility for the NHS in Scotland and the introduction of new laws (legislation) related to health. The duty (tax) paid on alcohol and cigarettes rises almost annually and possession of drugs such as heroin carries heavy penalties.

Smoking legislation

In a bid to reduce the number of people who smoke in Scotland, especially young people, laws have been introduced to restrict smoking. Health warnings are now clearly given on cigarette packets to highlight the dangers of smoking and cigarette companies cannot publicly advertise their products.

Smoking, Health and Social Care (Scotland) Act 2005

- It has been illegal in Scotland to smoke in the majority of enclosed public places since 2006. England followed suit in 2007.

Tobacco and Primary Medical Services (Scotland) Act 2010

- People must be at least 18 years old to buy tobacco products.
- Tobacco products cannot be openly displayed in larger shops etc.
- Vending machines cannot sell tobacco products.
- Packs of ten cigarettes will eventually be phased out.

South of Scotland Liberal Democrat MSP Jim Hume wants to introduce a Bill to the Scottish Parliament that would also introduce a ban on smoking in vehicles with children present. He is being supported by organisations including ASH Scotland and the British Lung Foundation.

In 2011, a Scottish study suggested that the air quality inside a smoker's car was comparable to industrial smog in cities such as Beijing or Moscow, even with the windows open.

THINGS TO DO AND THINK ABOUT

1   Why do you think the UK Government has delayed their plans to introduce plain packaging on cigarettes?
2   Why do you think women are more likely to seek medical help for health problems than men?

VIDEO LINK

Learn more about social exclusion by watching the video at www. brightredbooks.net/ N5ModernStudies.

FACT

The average life expectancy for females living in the most deprived areas of Scotland is 76.8 years compared to 84.2 years for those in the least deprived areas. Source: Audit Scotland, December 2012 (www.audit-scotland.gov.uk).

DON'T FORGET

Health is a devolved matter in Scotland.

DON'T FORGET

Laws can vary in different parts of the UK as a result of devolution.

NO SMOKING

ONLINE

Learn more about the smoking ban in Scotland at www.brightredbooks.net/ N5ModernStudies.

FACT

Despite the UK Government delaying the idea in July 2013, the Scottish Government remains committed to introducing plain cigarette packaging legislation. This new legislation would mean cigarette packets would all be the same colour, use the same font and carry a graphic warning.

TACKLING HEALTH INEQUALITIES 2

FACT

Lanarkshire-based Dr David Walker recently suggested that the Scottish Government should tax chocolate in the same way alcohol and cigarettes are taxed in a bid to tackle obesity.

ALCOHOL LEGISLATION

Scotland has many health and crime problems directly related to alcohol and binge drinking so laws have been introduced to make access to alcohol, especially for young people, more difficult and expensive.

In May 2012 the Scottish Government voted to introduce the Alcohol and Minimum Pricing (Scotland) Act. This will mean a minimum price of 50p per unit of alcohol sold in Scotland when it is finally introduced. This is an attempt to improve Scotland's health, make it more difficult for young people to access alcohol and reduce the crime rate associated with alcohol.

Since 2010, the Scottish Government has banned cheap alcohol promotions such as 'happy hours' and charged some retailers a social responsibility fee for the damage caused to communities by binge drinking in pubs and nightclubs etc. Based on independent research, which looked at the impact across the NHS, police, social services, the economy and on families, the total annual cost of alcohol misuse is estimated at between £2.48 billion and £4.64 billion – with a mid-point estimate of £3.56 billion.

Averaged across the population, the £3.56 billion figure means alcohol misuse could be costing every Scottish adult about £900 per year.

NHS Scotland

FACT

NHS (England) have recently announced an initiative offering shopping vouchers as rewards to encourage more women to breast feed their babies.

- Free prescriptions were introduced in Scotland in 2011. This means everyone can access the medication they need regardless of income.
- NHS Tayside's Quit4U programme offers pregnant women £12.50 per week in grocery vouchers if they quit smoking.
- Well woman and well man clinics offer free advice and support related to gender-specific health issues, e.g. prostate cancer checks for men.
- Free eye tests are available for all in Scotland.
- Free personal care is provided for the elderly in Scotland.

In 2011, Dr Daniel Chandler of NHS Dumfries and Galloway suggested that a minimum price per calorie should be introduced to tackle obesity.

Working together for a healthier Scotland

The Equally Well Report was published by the Ministerial Task Force on Health Inequalities in 2008 and reviewed in 2010. It highlighted Scotland's health inequalities problem and set targets to reduce them and increase life expectancy. The Scottish Parliament has introduced several Scotland-wide initiatives since then to tackle health inequalities.

- Schools are encouraged to become health-promoting schools and there has been an increased allocation of PE time and more active learning within the core curriculum to get young people more active.
- Nutritional standards have been set for school meals with limits on salt and sugar content and pupils are given incentives to pick the healthier options at lunchtimes. Some schools think that packed lunches should be banned in schools altogether, and to limit access to unhealthier options such as fast food, an age limit has been set in Scotland on when pupils can leave school premises at lunchtimes. These plans are known as the Hungry for Success initiative.
- People are encouraged to drink more water, eat at least five portions of fruit or vegetables per day and drink alcohol 'responsibly'.
- Health and wellbeing is an important part of all aspects of the Curriculum for Excellence.

Some MSPs would like to prohibit food company advertising that targets young people and introduce laws that ensure fast-food restaurants, takeaways etc. are not permitted near schools.

VOLUNTARY SECTOR

Voluntary organisations work to improve specific health problems in local communities. They put pressure on the government to change laws.

- Have a Heart Paisley works alongside the NHS with those at risk of heart problems to tackle risk factors.
- Voluntary Health Scotland is the national membership body for voluntary organisations working to improve health, tackle health inequalities or provide health care. They work with groups such as the Health and Social Care Alliance Scotland, Community Health Exchange, Community Food and Health Scotland, Voluntary Action Scotland, Scottish Healthy Living Alliance and Senscot.
- Oxfam carry out research and lobby the government on issues related to inequalities. See the *Our Economy* report published in 2013. They also support local organisations who work with vulnerable groups.
- The National Obesity Forum focuses on highlighting problems and tackling obesity from birth.
- UK-wide organisations such as the British Heart Foundation aim to highlight and tackle health inequalities.

LOCAL AUTHORITIES

The Local Government (Scotland) Act 1973 allows local authorities to introduce by-laws limiting the consumption of alcohol in public, for example with a few exceptions it is illegal to consume alcohol in a non-licensed public place within Glasgow City Council boundaries.

Scottish local authorities can provide free school meals for all Primary 1–3 pupils as well as free fruit and breakfast clubs to ensure a healthy breakfast, although recent financial cutbacks have threatened these programmes. Free school meals can be provided for some older children too.

Local authorities have responsibility for leisure services such as gyms, swimming pools and community centres. They often provide discounts for the use of facilities, especially for young people, to encourage more exercise.

DON'T FORGET

Community Planning Partnerships (CPPs) are responsible for bringing all the relevant organisations together locally and for taking the lead in tackling health inequalities.

PRIVATE SECTOR

The National Lottery has provided £300 million to set up healthy living centres in deprived areas of the UK to tackle issues such as heart disease, cancer and smoking.

Private health care and insurance

Some people choose to take out private health insurance policies with companies such as BMI Healthcare. Services covered can range from dentistry to surgery, but insurance policies can be very expensive. Some argue that due to the reduced demand, treatment can be quicker than on the NHS. The NHS have even paid for patients to be treated privately to reduce waiting lists!

Public-private partnership programmes

Under this initiative private companies build and run NHS hospitals on 'buy now pay later' schemes. In effect the government rents the buildings used as hospitals by the NHS. This has been a controversial programme as it results in paying back more than the project is worth over time. £6.7 billion has to be paid back over 30 years for 27 Scottish projects with an estimated value of only £1.28 billion.

FACT

Private firm Circle Health Care took full control of Hinchingbrooke Hospital in Cambridgeshire in 2011. This remains an NHS hospital but is fully managed by the company.

ONLINE TEST

Test your knowledge of tackling health inequalities at www.brightredbooks.net/N5ModernStudies.

THINGS TO DO AND THINK ABOUT

1. Outline the arguments for and against public–private partnership programmes.
2. Is your school a health-promoting school? How do you know?
3. Class debate: 'NHS Tayside's Quit4U initiative should be extended across Scotland.'

WEALTH INEQUALITIES IN GENDER AND RACE

WEALTH INEQUALITIES AND GENDER

There are approximately 32.2 million women in the UK, which is more than the male population of 31 million, yet there is a clear economic division between the genders, with women 'worse off' than men.

- Despite more women than men being employed in education, health and social work they are still more than twice as likely to be paid less than their male colleagues.
- **Gender segregation** in the workplace is a key cause of the gender pay gap and there are roles in society that are considered female and roles considered male.
- Women are more likely to work part-time (74% of all part-time workers are women) and have more gaps in their employment than men.
- Women make up the most of those in low-paid work: almost two-thirds (63%) of those earning £7 per hour or less are women. Women often cluster in roles relating to the five 'C's: caring, cashiering, catering, cleaning and clerical. These are often low-paid and temporary jobs.
- Women traditionally take on the role of primary care givers for children and that can have a significant impact on their income as they carry the burden of childcare costs, especially if they are lone parents (9 out of 10 lone parents are women). This is sometimes referred to as the 'motherhood penalty'.
- Women tend to be more dependent on welfare benefits than men.

The glass ceiling

This term refers to the invisible barrier that some women face in the workplace due to discrimination and stereotyping. Some women break through it but this glass ceiling can result in many women missing out on promotion and bonuses because of their commitments outside of work and prejudices inside work.

The glass ceiling exists when:

- Employers are reluctant to give positions of authority or responsibility to women as they fear they will not be committed enough or will take more time off than a male would.
- Women cannot compete for jobs with their male counterparts because they have taken career breaks or have gaps in their employment.
- Women cannot find successful female role models to look up to.
- A lack of flexibility in senior roles makes it difficult for women to juggle work and family life, e.g. no part-time work.
- Women cannot commit to the business life outside of the workplace and outwith normal working hours, e.g. on the golf course or in the pub.

GENDER AND EQUAL PAY CASE STUDY

In June 2013, 251 female employees of Dumfries and Galloway Council won an equal pay case at the Supreme Court. Female staff such as nursery nurses and classroom assistants argued they were entitled to the same pay and conditions as male manual workers such as refuse collectors, and after 7 years they won their case. Prior to this, male workers were entitled to bonuses and females were not and the local authority argued this was because the roles carried out were predominantly different and there was no 'real possibility' of the male workers doing the predominantly female roles in schools etc.

The local authority trade union Unison said the ruling could cost councils across Scotland £12m in compensation payments.

DON'T FORGET

There are successful and independently wealthy women in the UK, for example **entrepreneurs** such as Dragon's Den star and CEO Hilary Devey and Ultimo founder Michelle Mone.

VIDEO LINK

Check out the 'Celebrating International Women's Day' clip at www.brightredbooks.net/N5ModernStudies.

contd

Sex and Power Report 2013

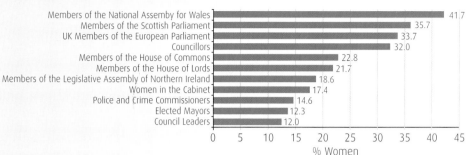

Women as a percentage of elected members of UK political institutions, January 2013.

WEALTH INEQUALITIES AND RACE

The term **'minority ethnic'** refers to those citizens who are not white. There is a UK population of roughly 5 million minority ethnics. This continues to rise, with the largest groups from Pakistani, Chinese, Indian and mixed backgrounds. Some areas of the UK have higher minority ethnic populations than others, e.g. London. Statistics show the following:

- There are more young black men unemployed than employed.
- Chinese graduates can expect to earn 25% less than their fellow white graduates.
- Those with an identifiably African- or Asian-origin name need to make nearly twice as many job applications to even get an interview for a job.
- There are higher rates of worklessness, unemployment and low pay within minority ethnic households.
- According to the Equality Outcomes and Mainstreaming Report 2013 there are 101 ethnic minority Scottish Government employees (representing only 1.4% of the total workforce).

Inequality exists between minority ethnic groups too, with those from Bangladeshi (50%) and Pakistani (45%) backgrounds suffering from higher poverty levels than not only whites (17%), but those from Indian (22%), African (25%) and Chinese (21%) backgrounds (source: The Joseph Rowntree Foundation, 2011).

Some inequalities exist for cultural reasons as there are high rates of lone parenthood within black African and black Caribbean communities, resulting in limited employment and reliance on benefits. Many Bangladeshi and Pakistani women are expected to stay at home rather than work or continue onto further education, which has an impact on household income. Some people from minority ethnic groups may be **first-generation immigrants**, which can result in language difficulties and qualifications not being recognised in the UK, limiting employment opportunities.

Discrimination and racism still exist, which creates inequalities:

- Direct racial discrimination – This is when people are treated differently because of their race.

- Indirect racial discrimination – This is where institutions and organisations may limit opportunities for certain groups with their rules and regulations, e.g. uniforms that may have an impact on cultural dress.

- Institutional racial discrimination – This occurs when an organisation's policies appear to have a negative impact on ethnic minorities. The Macpherson Report following the murder of black teenager Stephen Lawrence in 1993 found this to exist within the Metropolitan Police force.

THINGS TO DO AND THINK ABOUT

1 Create a spider diagram of the factors relating to the glass ceiling effect for women.
2 Inequalities in race are more obvious in some areas of the UK than others. Why is this?
3 Think of the reasons these inequalities exist. Can you think of any new policies the government could introduce to tackle inequalities?

ONLINE

Check out the site 'Counting Women In' for more at www.brightredbooks.net/ ModernStudies.

ONLINE

Check out the article 'Race inequalities exposed in public sector' at www. brightredbooks.net/ ModernStudies.

ONLINE

Get more statistics by reading the Family Resources Survey 2011/12 at www. brightredbooks.net/ N5ModernStudies.

DON'T FORGET

Not all people from minority ethnic groups live in poverty!

DON'T FORGET

Gender and race inequalities exist in health too.

FACT

One in four Pakistani men in Britain are taxi drivers or similar.

ONLINE TEST

Test your knowledge of this topic by taking the 'Wealth inequalities in gender and race' test at www.brightredbooks.net/ N5ModernStudies.

TACKLING WEALTH INEQUALITIES IN GENDER AND RACE

GOVERNMENT RESPONSES TO WEALTH INEQUALITIES

The UK Government has introduced legislation and initiatives to tackle inequalities in gender and race, but the current coalition government has been accused of not doing enough.

UK and European government responses

Previous laws such as the Equal Pay Act 1970, the Sex Discrimination Act 1975 and the Race Relations Act 1976 are now addressed under one piece of equal opportunities legislation.

The Equality Act 2010 makes it illegal to discriminate on the basis of:

- gender
- age
- disability
- sexual orientation
- pregnancy
- religion or belief
- race
- gender reassignment
- marriage and civil partnerships.

The Equality Act 2010 does not agree with the idea of different support for different social groups. It highlights the need to recognise that 'we are a nation of individuals', all with different needs and aspirations.

- The Equalities and Human Rights Commission (EHRC) has the job of trying to make sure the law works and promoting equality.

- The Ethnic Minority Employment Stakeholder Group (EMESG) is a government programme that ensures government initiatives focus on reducing the ethnic minority employment gap and encourages employers to tackle discrimination in the workplace.

Scottish Government responses to wealth inequalities

The Scottish Government has introduced the public sector equality duty, which encourages Scottish local authorities to:

- remove discrimination and harassment
- encourage equal opportunities between different groups
- promote positive relations between different groups.

Since its opening in 1999 the Scottish Parliament has tried to remove the gender imbalance amongst MSPs by implementing standard working hours, holidays around school term times and crèche provision. This has only been successful to a certain extent as the role of an MSP can still be very demanding outwith office hours.

POSITIVE ACTION/DISCRIMINATION

Positive action is a UK-wide policy that allows employers to address an imbalance in their workforce. This policy aims to reduce inequalities and increase opportunities for women and ethnic minorities specifically, but does not mean that one candidate will be automatically preferred to another. Workplace audits may be carried out to check if imbalances have been addressed and it is not enough to simply have equal numbers of men and women, there must be a balance within roles, e.g. not only men in high-paid management roles.

For example, if two candidates with the same skills and qualifications apply for a job and one is from a minority group and the other isn't, then positive discrimination will ensure that the candidate from the minority group will be offered the job.

contd

ONLINE

Learn more about the EHRC by following the link at www.brightredbooks.net/ModernStudies.

ONLINE

Read up on the Equalities Act 2010 by following the link at www.brightredbooks.net/ModernStudies.

FACT

Women-only shortlists for political representation are allowed until September 2030.

This is similar to American affirmative action programmes where employers are given quotas (specific numbers) they have to fill with people from ethnic minority backgrounds.

The Equality Act 2010 has not introduced quotas but some people are in favour of their introduction.

> Sheelagh Whittaker, non-executive director of Standard Life, told BBC Radio 4's Today programme that quotas were the answer. 'I am a big supporter of quotas. I believe that we will only have true equality when we have as many incompetent women in positions of power as incompetent men,' she said.

VOLUNTARY SECTOR RESPONSES TO WEALTH INEQUALITIES IN GENDER AND RACE

There are voluntary organisations that focus on highlighting inequalities and put pressure on the government for change.

The Fawcett Society

This is a campaigning organisation for women's equality and rights. They work to highlight and reduce gender inequalities in the UK.

The Joseph Rowntree Foundation

This organisation studies issues relating to poverty in the UK and publishes its findings on issues such as inequalities in race to encourage political debate.

Age UK

This voluntary organisation focuses on the needs of the elderly and highlights the specific needs of elderly minority groups.

THINGS TO DO AND THINK ABOUT

1   Outline the arguments for and against positive discrimination. Do you agree with this policy?

2   The Equality Act 2010 focuses on eliminating discrimination as a whole rather than on the specific issues such as gender and race. Why might some people disagree with this method of tackling inequalities?

3   Group investigation:

> Choose either gender or race.
>
> Choose either health or wealth inequalities.
>
> Create a **hypothesis** – what do you expect to find out?
>
> State at least two aims of your investigation.
>
> Investigate how your chosen group suffer from inequalities in the UK using at least two sources/research methods (internet, interviews, surveys, newspapers, TV programmes).
>
> Investigate specific groups and government policies that tackle your chosen inequality.
>
> Choose a method to present your findings, e.g. solo talk, group presentation, PowerPoint or poster.
>
> As other groups present their findings you should take notes.
>
> Finally, evaluate your investigation. How easy was it to find information? Were the sources you used appropriate? What might you have done differently?

ONLINE

Learn more about the Fawcett Society online (www.brightredbooks.net/N5ModernStudies).

VIDEO LINK

Learn more about the Joseph Rowntree Foundation online (www.brightredbooks.net/N5ModernStudies).

VIDEO LINK

Watch the 'Lunch clubs' clip at www.brightredbooks.net/N5ModernStudies to learn more about one of the schemes run by the Joseph Rowntree Foundation.

ONLINE

Learn more about Age UK online at www.brightredbooks.net/N5ModernStudies.

DON'T FORGET

There are many initiatives and programmes to tackle gender and race inequalities in health too.

ONLINE TEST

Test your knowledge of this topic by taking the 'Tackling wealth inequalities in gender and race' test at www.brightredbooks.net/N5ModernStudies.

WHAT IS CRIME?

Democratically elected MPs make laws that apply to the whole of the UK and since 1999 MSPs have had the power to make additional laws on devolved matters that only apply in Scotland, therefore a law may apply in Scotland, but not in England.

A crime is any act that breaks these laws.

ONLINE

Learn more about the Scottish Parliament online (www.brightredbooks.net/N5ModernStudies).

DON'T FORGET

These statistics are based on recorded crimes only but many crimes go unrecorded as people choose, for a variety of reasons, not to report them to the police.

ONLINE TEST

Test your knowledge of this topic by taking the 'What is crime?' test at www.brightredbooks.net/N5ModernStudies.

VIDEO LINK

Check out the clip 'Crime and public perception' at www.brightredbooks.net/N5ModernStudies.

TYPES OF CRIME

In order to monitor crime statistics, the Scottish Government places crimes into two groups, property crime and violent crime. They then split crimes further into five categories. This allows the government to decide where to focus when trying to tackle crime.

Crime group	Definition	Number of crimes recorded by police in Scotland, 2011–12
Non-sexual crimes of violence	Murder, attempted murder, serious assault, robbery, other	9,533
Sexual offences	Rape, attempted rape, sexual assault, prostitution, other	7,359
Crimes of dishonesty	Housebreaking, theft, shoplifting, fraud, other	154,337
Fire raising, vandalism etc.	Deliberately setting fires and damaging property	75,201
Other	Handling a weapon, drugs offences, traffic crime, public disorder, other	67,756

Source: Scottish Crime and Justice Survey, 2012.

The Scottish Crime and Justice Survey (SCJS) measures recorded crime in Scotland annually. Their findings have shown that young males are the most likely social group to be victims of crime and that the crime rate is higher in areas of social deprivation, for example in Glasgow, with 1019 crimes committed in 2011–12 per 10,000 of the population.

Before all Scottish police forces merged and became Police Scotland in 2013 the overall crime statistics for 2012–13 per force were as shown in the table. All forces showed a decrease in recorded crime from the previous year.

contd

Police force	Number of crimes in 2012–13
Central	14,056 (down 14%)
Dumfries & Galloway	5,350 (down 11%)
Grampian	25,866 (down 12%)
Fife	15,230 (down 15%)
Lothian & Borders	48,789 (down 13%)
Northern Constabulary	11,355 (down 16%)
Strathclyde	133,601 (down 14%)
Tayside	17,806 (down 6%)

Source: Scottish Government.

Crimes tend to happen in larger cities, near to popular drinking areas and nightspots, and in socially deprived areas.

Serious organised crime

Serious organised crime can involve a range of activities from drug dealing and counterfeiting to prostitution and human trafficking, where vulnerable people are sold into forms of slavery. Organised crime groups can span the world and use the money they make from things like pirate DVDs to fund more serious crimes like human trafficking.

White-collar crime

The term 'white-collar crime' covers any crime that was committed for financial gain by 'a person of respectability and high social status in the course of his occupation'. Examples of white-collar crime are fraud, embezzlement, bribery, insider trading, money laundering and cyber crime.

Blue-collar crime

People in relatively unskilled occupations or who are unemployed and socially disadvantaged may commit crimes such as housebreaking, shoplifting or vandalism. These types of crimes tend to happen more often than white-collar crimes and are more obvious. They are known as blue-collar crimes.

New crime

As society and technology change, crimes change too. Crimes such as cyber bullying, where people are abused via the internet, and hate crimes, where people are targeted because of their race, religion or sexuality, have been on the increase recently. New laws have been introduced to tackle these crimes and try to prevent them.

 VIDEO LINK

Check out the video 'Mobile phone technology to help tackle crime' at www.brightredbooks.net/N5ModernStudies.

 FACT

Teachers in Scotland are increasingly being subjected to cyber bullying from pupils. Sixty-eight per cent have received unpleasant e-mails, 26% have been the subject of abuse on websites and 28% have received abusive text messages.

THINGS TO DO AND THINK ABOUT

1 Why might some people not report crimes to the police?

2 What types of crimes are more likely to be committed by young people?

3 Explain the difference between blue- and white-collar crime.

4 Why does criminal law regularly have to be reviewed and updated?

CAUSES OF CRIME

It is not easy to explain why people commit crime as there are many causes. People have to be accountable for their actions, but it is clear that some people are more likely to commit crime than others.

ONLINE

Check out the article 'What causes crime?' for more on this debate: www.brightredbooks.net/N5ModernStudies.

INDIVIDUALIST VERSUS COLLECTIVIST THEORY

There are two main theories of why people commit crime. Individualists believe that a person chooses to commit a crime and they should be punished for it. They feel that stronger punishments would result in less crime. Collectivists believe that poor social conditions, such as poor housing and unemployment, cause crime. They feel that if people are employed and happy, they are unlikely to commit crime.

Individualists believe that crimes are committed based on a rational choice made by an individual, while collectivists believe that crime is a result of poor social circumstances that need to be addressed by the government.

POVERTY AND SOCIAL EXCLUSION

Local authorities with large cities and urban areas tend to have higher crime rates than more rural areas. Many of these areas are considered deprived and Glasgow City Council has more areas of deprivation than any other local authority in Scotland, as well as the highest crime rate of all council areas.

In some areas there is a lack of facilities, especially for young people. This can lead to boredom, which can lead to crime.

VIDEO LINK

Check out the clip 'Residents transform housing estates to reduce crime' at www. brightredbooks.net/N5ModernStudies.

DRUGS AND ALCOHOL

In 2011–12, 124 people were accused of homicide (murder) in Scotland. Eighty-two per cent were reported to have been drunk and/or under the influence of drugs at the time. Almost all female prisoners admitted to Cornton Vale prison test positive for drugs on admission. People who are addicted to drugs may commit further crimes to get access to them.

According to the SCJS 2010–11 victims perceived the offender to have been under the influence of alcohol in 63% of recorded violent crimes and to have taken drugs in 34% of recorded violent crimes.

GREED

Not all crimes are committed by those in poverty. Some crimes are committed by those from affluent backgrounds who want more money and think they can 'get away with it' and no-one will notice.

PEER PRESSURE

Many people, especially young people, feel pressure to 'fit in'. This may lead to people carrying out crimes they think might impress others or shoplifting items they cannot afford to buy, such as the latest mobile phone or gadget.

LACK OF POSITIVE ROLE MODELS

Some people may come from poor family backgrounds and have no positive role models in their lives to look up to. In some areas the people who are viewed as successful and influential are those who deal drugs or run gangs as few will go on to further education or embark on professional careers. Young people whose lives lack family structure may seek support from other places such as gangs. The gang becomes the family and they are often involved in crime.

Some young people may not be encouraged to attend school, meaning they have a lack of structure in their lives and a lack of opportunities later in life. Many children grow up in substance-abusing households. They are often neglected, which can cause long-term psychological and emotional damage. Many young offenders who come from 'troubled families' show a lack of empathy and can appear very angry. A lack of discipline in childhood can also be a factor and criminal parents often lead to their children to crime.

EDUCATION

It is often claimed that low literacy is related to unemployment, a lack of aspiration, poor physical and mental health, and/or great deprivation, which can lead to crime. Children who regularly truant or are excluded from school tend to have only basic literacy skills so it is thought that literacy improvement is a key part of any crime prevention strategy.

UK figures have shown that 25% of young offenders have reading skills below those of the average 7-year-old and 60% of the prison population have difficulties with basic literacy skills.

2011 ENGLISH RIOTS

In August 2011, a young black male named Mark Duggan was shot and killed by police in London. They had tried to arrest him and an illegal gun was found at the scene of the incident. Mark Duggan's family and supporters took to the streets to peacefully protest about the shooting but this soon escalated to full-scale rioting across several areas of London. Police found it difficult to deal with the increasingly violent crowds and the rioting spread to other UK cities such as Manchester.

When the riots eventually ended, five people had died, many people had lost their homes due to fires and businesses had been looted. The total cost of the riots is difficult to calculate but it is estimated at over half a billion pounds.

> *The Guardian* carried out a survey called 'Reading the Rioters'. They interviewed 270 rioters from ages 13 to 57 and from a range of ethnic backgrounds. Their findings showed that the majority of rioters interviewed were young males (only 21% females), poorer than the country at large, with low levels of educational attainment. Their ethnicities varied between areas and approximately 76% of those interviewed had previous convictions.
>
> Many of those interviewed stated issues such as unemployment, government budget cuts and recession, the growing divide between the rich and poor in the UK, and the lack of educational or entrepreneurial opportunities for young people, particularly those from ethnic minority groups, as reasons for participating in the 2011 riots. Others cited reasons such as retaliation against an institutionally racist and disrespectful police force.

THINGS TO DO AND THINK ABOUT

1   Create a spider diagram of the main causes of crime.

2   Carry out an investigation and present your findings on the causes of the 2011 riots.

FACT

A MORI 2003 survey found that education (45%) alongside better parenting (59%) and a larger police force (55%) were believed to be among the best ways to reduce crime.

DON'T FORGET

It is important to remember that it is usually a combination of factors that leads to crime.

ONLINE TEST

How much do you know about the causes of crime? Take the test at www.brightredbooks.net/N5ModernStudies.

VIDEO LINK

Have a look at the news report on the riots at www.brightredbooks.net/N5ModernStudies.

FACT

These events have been nicknamed the 'Blackberry riots' because of the use of mobile devices and social media in their organisation.

IMPACT OF CRIME

The SCJS states that one in six adults over the age of 16 was a victim of a crime between 2011 and 2012. In addition, 5.9% of adults were estimated to have been a victim of property crime and 3% of adults had been a victim of violent crime.

Even crimes that are assumed to be victimless, such as tax avoidance, have a significant impact on communities as that money could have been spent to improve deprived areas.

WHY ARE SOME PEOPLE MORE LIKELY TO BECOME VICTIMS OF CRIME?

ONLINE

Check out the 'What is hate crime?' link at www.brightredbooks.net/N5ModernStudies.

VIDEO LINK

Watch the clip on stopping hate crime: www.brightredbooks.net/N5ModernStudies.

FACTFILE (based on 2011–12 SCJS)

- Males are slightly more likely to be the victim of a crime (18%) compared to females (17%).
- 16- to 24-year-olds had the highest risk of being a victim of violent crime compared to 9% of those over 60.
- The risk of property crime was higher for adults living in the 15% most deprived areas (21%) compared with those living in the rest of Scotland (17%).
- **Sectarianism** features in many crimes.
- Hate crimes are on the increase against ethnic minorities. There has been an increase in Islamaphobia since 2001.

Main findings on hate crime			
Crime types	2010/11	2011/12	Percentage change
Race	4,178	4,518	+7.53%
Religious aggravation	695	897	+29.06%
Sexual orientation	447	652	+45.86%
Aggravation of disability	48	68	+41.66%
Aggravation of transgender identity	14	16	+14.29%
TOTAL	5,385	6,151	+14.22%

Source: Crown Office and Procurator Fiscal

IMPACT ON INDIVIDUALS

The impact of crime on individuals can vary. Some people can seem fine whilst others have severe reactions. How people react can depend on:

- the type of crime committed and how 'serious' it was
- whether you know the person who committed the crime
- the support received from family, friends, the police etc
- personal history

Victims can struggle with the idea that a crime was committed deliberately by another person, unlike an accident, where there is no harm intended. Victims can feel powerless and vulnerable. This can be especially difficult to deal with if the crime is repeated or ongoing, which is often the case with domestic violence or racial harassment. It's also a big issue for hate crime victims who have been singled out because of who they are.

Physical

Victims who have been physically attacked may suffer scars or disabilities as a result. People can feel ill or be unable to sleep.

contd

When someone is murdered it is not just the victim who suffers, their families and friends do too.

Social and emotional

The social and emotional impact of crime or the fear of crime can be significant. People may become too scared to leave their homes, meaning they cannot work or attend school. People can become depressed or socially excluded and in some cases individuals can suffer from post-traumatic stress disorder.

Economic

Young people who commit crimes will have a criminal record for the rest of their lives and tend to do less well at school. This has an impact on their opportunities and job prospects later in life. People can lose money or belongings due to crime. Replacing items that have been stolen or damaged can be very expensive.

IMPACT ON COMMUNITIES

The broken window theory

This theory suggests that a broken window left unrepaired will make a building look uncared for or abandoned and soon attract vandals to break all the other windows. If areas are covered in graffiti and left damaged it sends a message that no-one cares and crime is acceptable, so crime rates will rise. Areas look run down and depressing with broken windows and graffiti so people will not want to live or work there. If an area looks run down, house values will fall, leaving people stuck in certain areas and creating derelict buildings.

Unemployment and lack of investment

If companies fear crime they are less likely to invest and create jobs in certain areas. These areas then become stereotyped and the cycle continues. This also means fewer local opportunities for young people.

Social exclusion

In crime blackspots people may feel unsafe and avoid socialising. This means no sense of community is created and people keep themselves to themselves. Gangs or young teams may instil fear of public spaces in some areas. This tends to happen in the most deprived areas.

Drug and alcohol abuse

If people feel depressed because of a lack of opportunities or a fear of crime they may abuse drugs or alcohol as they look for a distraction.

Increased police presence

Areas with high crime rates tend to have a significantly higher police presence than other areas as police try to tackle the issue. There may also be a large number of CCTV cameras, leading to people, especially youths, feeling they are not trusted and are targeted.

Increased security

In areas with high crime rates people may feel the need to take expensive security measures and prices may be increased in shops etc to cover the costs.

THINGS TO DO AND THINK ABOUT

Carry out a local crime survey in your area. You should aim to find out:
- what types of crime happen in your area
- why people think these particular crimes take place
- who is blamed for these crimes
- what can be done to tackle these crimes.

Think carefully about who and what you'll ask and be prepared to present your findings.

ONLINE

For more on the impact of crime on victims, check out the link at www.brightredbooks.net/N5ModernStudies.

VIDEO LINK

Learn more about the broken window theory by watching the clip at www.brightredbooks.net/N5ModernStudies.

ONLINE TEST

How much do you know about the impact of crime? Take the test at www.brightredbooks.net/N5ModernStudies.

DON'T FORGET

Many crimes that affect both individuals and communities are the result of anti-social behaviour.

FACT

According to the 2010–11 SCJS 31% of adults said they felt unsafe walking alone in their local area after dark (very unsafe 10%, a bit unsafe 21%). Females were more likely than males to report feeling unsafe (44% of females compared with 17% of males).

TACKLING CRIME IN SCOTLAND

The Scottish Government is committed to making Scotland a safer place and believes strongly in crime prevention as well as tough sentencing. The Global Study on Homicide, published in 2012, showed Glasgow to have a particularly high murder rate of 3.3 per 100,000 people compared to 1.6 per 100,000 people in London. There are various organisations in Scotland that aim to improve these statistics.

ONLINE

Learn more about Police Scotland by viewing their website (www.brightredbooks.net/N5ModernStudies).

POLICE SCOTLAND – PROTECT, PRESERVE AND PREVENT

In April 2013, eight Scottish police forces, the Scottish Organised Crime and Drug Enforcement Agency and the Association of Chief Police Officers in Scotland merged to create Police Scotland, which takes responsibility to protect the public and property, preserve order and prevent crimes taking place. Major crimes are investigated by the Specialist Crime Division.

Protect people and property	Arrest suspects, officers 'on the beat', interview suspects and witnesses, investigate crimes, stop and search
Preserve order	Presence at football matches, protests etc., community officers, managing traffic
Prevent crime	Work with community groups, visit schools, introduce initiatives, campus officers

FACT

Two officers, 23-year-old PC Nicola Hughes and 32-year-old PC Fiona Bone, were killed in an incident in Manchester after being sent to check out a routine house burglary report. Dale Cregan shot both officers and threw grenades.

Some recent police initiatives include:

- Blue Light discos in schools
- Doorstep – tackling doorstep crime in North Lanarkshire
- Knife Amnesty
- Hate Crime
- Autism Awareness
- Young Runaways
- Play safe, Home safe
- Anti-Sectarianism and Unacceptable Behaviour
- Operation Ultraviolet – drug raids in Central Scotland in 2009.

Police Scotland has a network of armed response units across the country but the majority of officers only carry batons, CS spray and spit masks, and wear stab vests for protection. The pressure group Protect the Protectors has campaigned for the police to be armed with guns for protection.

The Violence Reduction Unit

The Violence Reduction Unit (VRU) works alongside Police Scotland and the Scottish Government to tackle violence in Scotland. They have introduced various projects, e.g. Community Initiative to Reduce Violence (CIRV) – which ran between 2009 and 2011 in Glasgow's east end and reduced gang violence by almost 50% – and Mentors in Violence Prevention.

FACT

The VRU has introduced the Braveheart Industries project, which is based on an American project used in Los Angeles. This is a social enterprise project that aims to help former gang members in Scotland turn their lives around by accessing jobs and education.

SCOTTISH GOVERNMENT INITIATIVES – SAFER SCOTLAND

The Scottish Government has set up several initiatives to promote Safer Scotland:

- Community safety units – aim to reduce antisocial behaviour and violence, and promote positive behaviour through the CashBack for Communities programme.
- CashBack for Communities – the Proceeds of Crime Act 2002 means the government can seize any assets it believes to have been gained though criminal activities. It then uses this money to fund community projects (aimed at young people) to prevent crime. Over £50 million was recovered in 2007 and this initiative has benefited over 600,000 young people.
- Increased use of CCTV.
- Reducing Reoffending Programme – introduced into Scottish prisons. The Scottish Government works alongside community projects and charities to reduce reoffending.

ONLINE TEST

How much do you know about tackling crime in Scotland? Take the test at www.brightredbooks.net/N5ModernStudies.

contd

COMMUNITY PROJECTS AND CHARITIES

Local councils, charities and communities often introduce initiatives to tackle particular crime issues in their areas.

- FARE (Family Action in Rogerfield and Easterhouse) – anti-gang projects used alongside CIRV.
- Medics against violence – volunteer healthcare professionals deliver anti-violence lessons in schools.
- Fresh Start with Forth Valley College – for those on community service.
- Includem – mentoring programmes for young offenders in Glasgow.
- Action for Children – Dundee Alternative to Custody Programme, Tayside Treatment Service.
- Barnardo's Unlock – young offenders work in charity shops and have the opportunity to complete a Youth Achievement Certificate. They may get help whilst in custody to write CVs etc.

Glasgow City Council has introduced neighbourhood improvement volunteers, who aim to make communities safe and cleaner; graffiti teams and Nite Zones, which make it safer for those queuing for transportation such as taxis at night.

CLOSED CIRCUIT TELEVISION

More than 4000 closed circuit television (CCTV) cameras monitor Scotland's cities and towns.

Nick Pickles, director of the civil liberties campaign group Big Brother Watch, insisted that CCTV was 'lousy' at deterring crime.

He said: 'The public would be far safer if the money was spent on street lighting, proper policing and actually punishing criminals when they are caught, rather than giving them a slap on the wrist and putting them back on the streets.

'In too many towns we now have a CCTV on every street corner, yet never see a police officer there. The public are treated as suspects to be monitored by faceless council officials, yet we are no safer walking the streets as a result.'

However, the cameras are seen as an invaluable tool in the fight against crime. In Edinburgh alone, figures show CCTV resulted in 1806 camera-assisted arrests.

A Scottish Government spokeswoman pointed out that recorded crime was now at its lowest level in 37 years.

'Fear of crime is down and more people are feeling safer in their neighbourhoods.'

She added: 'CCTV has played an important role in making our streets safer by helping our police and prosecuting authorities catch criminals and tackle antisocial behaviour.'

Source: *The Scotsman,* 2012

KNIFE CRIME IN SCOTLAND

It is an offence to carry or purchase most types of knife in Scotland if you are under 18, yet Scotland has a serious knife crime problem, particularly when alcohol is involved. Nearly half of all murders committed in Scotland in 2009–10 involved a sharp instrument..

The Scottish Government has introduced the 'No Knives, Better Lives' campaign, which works alongside Police Scotland to tackle knife crime. The campaign aims to increase anti-knife education and increase police stop-and-search powers in high crime areas. The maximum sentence for carrying a knife has also recently been increased to 5 years. .

Campaign for Change is an organisation that lobbies politicians to change laws and sentencing related to knife crime in Scotland. It would like a mandatory 20-year sentence for those found guilty of murder using a knife and for greater consistency in sentencing across Scotland.

THINGS TO DO AND THINK ABOUT

1 Group task: Should the police be armed? Your group should research the issue, draw a conclusion and present your findings to the rest of the class.
2 'Increasing the number of CCTV cameras across Scotland would reduce crime.' Do you agree with this statement? Explain your answer.

VIDEO LINK

Check out the arguments for and against the use of CCTV at www.brightredbooks.net/N5ModernStudies.

VIDEO LINK

Have a look at the clips on knife crime at www.brightredbooks.net/N5ModernStudies.

FACT

Statistics show that young men are more likely to be involved in knife crime than girls and that it is linked to **gang culture**. Gang members in Scottish cities like Glasgow and Edinburgh may carry knives to deliberately do harm to others, to protect themselves from rival gangs or because of peer pressure.

ALCOHOL, DRUGS AND TRAFFIC LAWS

IMPACT OF ALCOHOL AND CRIME AND THE LAW

Alcohol has been shown to be a contributory factor in many crimes in Scotland and issues relating to alcohol (health issues, clear-ups, violence, etc.) cost the Scottish Government £727.1 million per year.

- Alcohol was a factor for half of those accused of homicide in Scotland in 2003.
- 426 people were caught over the drink-driving limit in Scotland during Christmas 2010.
- Half the prisoners in Scotland's jails (70% of young offenders) were drunk at the time of their offence.
- 70% of assaults presenting at A&E are alcohol related.
- 1 in 20 drunken offences results in a conviction.
- The cost of alcohol related crime to the criminal justice and emergency services is around £385m per year.
- Domestic violence incidents are often alcohol related.

Source: Alcohol Focus Scotland

Anyone caught selling alcohol to or buying alcohol for someone under the age of 18 faces prosecution.

In May 2012 the Scottish Government voted to introduce the Alcohol and Minimum Pricing (Scotland) Act. This requires a minimum price of 50p per unit of alcohol sold in Scotland. This is an attempt to improve Scotland's health and reduce the crime rate.

The Local Government (Scotland) Act 1973 means that local authorities can introduce by-laws specific to one area, e.g. it is illegal to drink outside in public in Glasgow but not in Edinburgh.

The Licensing (Scotland) Act 2005 came into force in 2009 and introduced laws to tackle underage drinking such as 'no proof, no sale' meaning if someone cannot prove they are over 18 with ID, such as a passport, the sale can be refused. In 2010 cheap alcohol promotions such as happy hours were banned in Scotland and venues selling alcohol now have a responsibility not to serve drunk people. Some alcohol retailers have been charged a social responsibility fee to cover the costs of alcohol misuse.

Police can take alcohol from underage drinkers in public places, and from those over 18 who are suspected of supplying alcohol to underage drinkers.

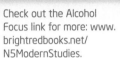

ONLINE

Check out the Alcohol Focus link for more: www.brightredbooks.net/N5ModernStudies.

DON'T FORGET

Alcohol minimum pricing only applies in Scotland.

IMPACT OF DRUGS ON CRIME AND THE LAW

Should cannabis be legalised? ✔ ✘

Illegal drug classifications 2013

Class A	Cocaine, heroin, ecstasy
Class B	Cannabis, speed, amphetamines
Class C	GHB, tranquillizers, ketamine

FOR	AGAINST
Some forms are stronger than others	Less harmful than alcohol or tobacco
Linked to mental illness	Dispute over link to mental illness
Gateway drug to harder drugs	Waste of police time

A total of 35,157 drug crimes were recorded in 2011–12, up from 34,347 in 2010–11. This was the first rise in recorded drug crimes in Scotland since 2008–09. In 2011–12 there were 28,326 crimes of possession of drugs recorded compared to 26,960 in 2010–11.

Penalties vary depending on the drug classification and the amount someone is in possession of. In the eyes of the law, dealing drugs is considered more serious than simply being in possession of some drugs.

FACT

Cannabis was reclassified as a Class C drug in 2004 and reclassified back to a Class B drug in 2005.

contd

Proposed changes to drug laws

- Target those who grow and supply cannabis.
- Ban the sale of drug-taking equipment.
- Harsher sentencing for those caught supplying near schools.

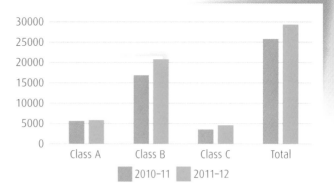

Number of drug seizures by Scottish police forces, by class of drug, for 2010–11 and 2011–12 (Scottish Government statistics).

SMOKING LAWS IN SCOTLAND

The Scottish Government is trying to improve Scotland's health by introducing tougher laws on smoking. This is targeted at stopping young people from taking up smoking.

Smoking, Health and Social Care (Scotland) Act 2005

- It is illegal in Scotland to smoke in the majority of enclosed public places.

Tobacco and Primary Medical Services (Scotland) Act 2010

- Must be at least 18 years old to buy tobacco products in Scotland.
- Tobacco products cannot be openly displayed in larger shops etc.
- Vending machines cannot sell tobacco products.
- Packs of ten cigarettes will be phased out.

THE ROAD TRAFFIC ACT 1988 (UK-WIDE)

This covers many aspects of driving and makes certain behaviours that are considered dangerous illegal. Under this legislation drivers must have valid licences and insurance, and wear seatbelts.

Driving under the influence

The Road Traffic Act states that the amount of alcohol a person can have in their bloodstream and legally drive is 80 mg per 100 ml. The Scottish Government has discussed reducing this to 50 mg and since the introduction of the Scotland Act 2012 it has the power to change the limit. Driving under the influence of alcohol can lead to up to six months in prison or a fine of up to £5000, and anyone convicted of death by dangerous driving when under the influence of drugs faces a maximum sentence of 15 years. Police can now issue £100 on-the-spot fines for careless driving offences such as speeding, tailgating, not wearing a seatbelt or using a hand-held mobile device whilst behind the wheel.

Speeding and totting up

Speeding is the most common traffic offence. The Road Traffic Act means drivers caught speeding will be given from three to six penalty points on their licence. In some cases, the driver can be disqualified from driving altogether. If a driver receives 12 or more points within three years they will be disqualified from driving for a minimum period of six months.

Using a mobile phone

Using a mobile phone whilst driving can result in three penalty points and a £100 fine.

Careless or dangerous driving

If a driver is charged with careless or dangerous driving they can be disqualified for a minimum period of one year and ordered to re-sit their driving test. A court can also impose large fines and even a prison sentence.

VIDEO LINK

Check out the clip on smoking legislation in Lanarkshire for more: www.brightredbooks.net/N5ModernStudies.

FACT

Despite the UK Parliament rejecting the idea, the Scottish Government remains committed to introducing plain packaging on all cigarette packets.

FACT

The Scotland Act 2012 gave the Scottish Government new powers over speed limits on Scottish roads.

ONLINE TEST

How much do you know about alcohol, drugs and traffic laws? Take the test at www.brightredbooks.net/N5ModernStudies.

THINGS TO DO AND THINK ABOUT

Class debate topics:
- Cannabis should be legalised.
- A zero alcohol limit for drivers should be introduced.
- The age limit for purchasing alcohol should be increased to 21.

THE COURT SYSTEM IN SCOTLAND

All courts in Scotland are organised by the Scottish Court Service (SCS), which is led by the Scottish Government. They deal with either criminal or civil cases. If someone is tried under criminal law, the Scottish Government accuses them of breaking a law of Scotland, whereas if a case is civil it involves a dispute between individuals or organisations.

DON'T FORGET

Scotland has its own court system, which is different from the rest of the UK.

The High Court of Justiciary.

ONLINE

Find out more about the court system in Scotland online at www. brightredbooks.net/ N5ModernStudies.

FACT

The last person to be hanged for murder in Scotland was Henry John Burnett in Aberdeen on 15 August 1963.

VIDEO LINK

Check out the clips about the death penalty at www.brightredbooks.net/ N5ModernStudies for more.

ONLINE

Have a look at the BBC Ethics guide on the death penalty for more: www. brightredbooks.net/ ModernStudies.

PROSECUTION OF A CRIME

When someone is accused of a crime, the police submit the evidence to the Crown Office and Procurator Fiscal Service (COPFS), who decide whether or not to **prosecute**.

There are two types of criminal court procedure, solemn and summary. In solemn procedure a jury of 15 members of the public listen to the evidence and decide on the **verdict**. A judge is also present and he or she decides on any sentence that may be issued.

There are three main criminal courts in Scotland: the High Court of Justiciary, the Sheriff Court and Justice of the Peace Courts.

THE HIGH COURT OF JUSTICIARY

This is the supreme criminal court in Scotland and it deals with the most serious crimes, such as murder (homicide), culpable homicide, rape, armed robbery, treason and serious sexual offences, particularly those involving children.

The High Court has unlimited sentencing powers such as 'life' (between 15 and 35 years) imprisonment or an unlimited fine. Prior to 1965, the High Court had the power to issue the death penalty (capital punishment). Those found guilty of murder would be hanged. The death penalty was officially abolished for murder in 1965 but it wasn't until 1998 that it was abolished for the crime of treason!

Arguments for the death penalty	Arguments against the death penalty
Current methods of execution such as lethal injections are reliable, quick and painless (more humane than in the past).	There have been instances where lethal injection has been slow and painful.
If a person takes someone's life they deserve to die.	Life in prison causes more suffering.
It acts as a deterrent to those who may commit serious crimes.	It does not act as a deterrent, for example the US state of Texas currently uses the death penalty and executed 15 people by lethal injection in 2012 alone.
Some murderers are incapable of being rehabilitated.	It goes against basic human rights.
It costs the Scottish Government up to £40,000 per year to imprison one person. Life could mean 35 years, which is £1,400,000! That tax money could be better spent on other devolved matters such as healthcare.	Guilty verdicts can be wrong. Innocent people may be executed.

THE SHERIFF COURT

Currently, 49 Sheriff Courts represent districts in Scotland, but this number is to be reduced to 39 between November 2013 and January 2015, and only 21 of the remaining Sheriff Courts will deal with solemn cases. These closures will also affect nine Justice of the Peace Courts that use the same facilities. Cases that would have been heard in these courts will be referred to remaining courts in other areas, e.g. Dingwall Sheriff Court cases will now be dealt with in Inverness and Cumbernauld Justice of the Peace business will now go to Coatbridge.

contd

Glasgow Sheriff Court deals with the highest number of cases in Scotland. This court hears both criminal and civil cases, and uses both solemn and summary procedure.

The Sheriff Court deals with crimes such as theft, assault, soliciting, possession of drugs and appeals from a Children's Hearing.

Under solemn procedure, sheriffs can issue sentences of up to 5 years in prison or an unlimited fine. Under summary procedure, a sheriff can fine someone up to £10,000 or sentence them to up to 12 months in prison.

There is also a range of **non-custodial sentences** that can be issued by the sheriff. These are addressed later in this book.

The types of civil cases the Sheriff Court can deal with are separation, divorce or dissolution of a civil partnership, adoption or custody.

JUSTICE OF THE PEACE COURTS

This court replaced the District Court in 2007 and is a lay court (business can be carried out anywhere) where a Justice of the Peace (JP) presides with the support of a legally qualified clerk. These courts deal with minor offences such as breach of the peace, being drunk and disorderly, and traffic offences.

A JP can issue a maximum **custodial sentence** of up to 60 days and a fine of up to £2500.

THE COURT OF SESSION

This is Scotland's supreme civil court and it sits in Edinburgh. The Court of Session can be used as a court of appeal and is headed by a Lord President. This court recently rejected an appeal brought by the Scotch Whisky Association and other wine and spirits producers against the Scottish Government's new alcohol minimum pricing legislation.

ONLINE

For more, check out the 'Scottish courts' link at www.brightredbooks.net/ModernStudies.

DON'T FORGET

Since 2011, the Scottish Government has had an SNP majority, with Kenny MacAskill as Justice Secretary.

ONLINE TEST

Test your knowledge by taking the 'The court system in Scotland' test at www.brightredbooks.net/N5ModernStudies.

THINGS TO DO AND THINK ABOUT

1   Explain the difference between summary and solemn procedure.

2   Create spider diagrams of the courts in Scotland. Include the types of case each court hears and examples of crimes, who is present throughout the case and the maximum sentencing powers.

3   The Scottish Government (led by the SNP) plan to reduce the number of Sheriff Courts in Scotland has been criticised by organisations like the Law Society of Scotland and political parties such as the Scottish Liberal Democrats and Scottish Labour.

In pairs, discuss the issue and agree on the following:
    a   at least two reasons why the Scottish Government wishes to close these Sheriff Courts
    b   at least three reasons why other parties and organisations are against the closures.

4   Death penalty survey.
    a   Get into a group of three or four and create a survey of at least two questions based on the issue of the use of the death penalty, e.g. should the death penalty be an available sentence in Scotland for convicted murderers?
                        Yes   No   Don't know
    b   Survey as many people as possible outside school and note their answers. Try to ask at least five different people.
    c   Collate your group's findings and present them in the form of a poster, using graphs and pie charts to display statistics.
    d   Finally, evaluate your survey:
        • Were the questions and people you asked appropriate?
        • State two good things and two bad things about using a survey for research.
        • Are there any other methods you could have used to find out information?
        • Might they have worked better?

VERDICTS AND SENTENCING IN SCOTLAND

VIDEO LINK

Watch this news clip about a famous not proven verdict: www.brightredbooks.net/N5ModernStudies.

ONLINE

Read the article "Not proven' fixture of Scots law set for review' at www.brightredbooks.net/N5ModernStudies.

DON'T FORGET

The not proven verdict only exists in Scotland.

ONLINE

Investigate the role of the not proven verdict in the trial of Francis Auld for the murder of Amanda Duffy in Hamilton in 1992 at www.brightredbooks.net/ModernStudies

FACT

In March 2011, the Double Jeopardy (Scotland) Act was introduced, which allowed a person to be re-tried for the same crime if there is 'compelling new evidence'.

VERDICTS

There are three verdicts/decisions available in Scottish courts.

Verdict	Definition
Not guilty	Based on the evidence the accused did not commit any crime and is free to go
Guilty	Based on the evidence the accused committed a crime 'beyond any reasonable doubt'
Not proven	There is suspicion of guilt but not enough evidence to convict – the accused is free to go

The not proven verdict is controversial as it suggests that there is some suspicion of guilt but the evidence provided does not prove guilt 'beyond all reasonable doubt'.

Arguments for not proven	Arguments against not proven
Allows judges and juries to express reasonable doubt	Evidence suggests guilt
Continues to be used in Scottish courts	May leave a permanent mark on the character of innocent people
It may be more satisfactory for victims and witnesses by reflecting the absence of necessary proof without casting doubt on their evidence	Traumatic for victims and families of victims
Juries can be unfairly influenced	Confusing and pointless

As Scotland has its own legal system it has its own range of sentences (punishments) that can be issued to those found guilty of crimes in Scottish courts.

ENTERING A PLEA

Before a case goes to trial the accused has the option of entering a **plea**. This means the accused can state whether they are guilty or not guilty of the crime or crimes they are accused of.

If the accused pleads guilty a trial is not necessary and the sentence issued may be more lenient than if a trial had gone ahead. The accused can also plead guilty at any time during a trial to try and reduce their sentence.

If the accused pleads not guilty then a trial will go ahead if the Procurator Fiscal feels it is necessary.

Barlinnie Prison.

CUSTODIAL SENTENCING

People accused of serious crimes may be sent to prison to await their trial. This is called being on remand.

If a person is found guilty of a serious crime they may be taken into custody. This means they may be forced to spend time in a prison or a young offenders' institution (discussed later in this book) run by the Scottish Prison Service (SPS). A judge can sentence someone to life in prison, which can mean anything between 13 and 35 years. At present, anyone convicted of a murder automatically receives a life sentence, with guidance to judges to impose a minimum 16-year punishment on those who kill with a knife.

If prisoners are well behaved, they may be given **parole** and released early or be given a non-custodial sentence for the remainder of their time. Some prisoners may be released on a life licence with conditions attached, which if broken will mean a return to prison.

NON-CUSTODIAL SENTENCING

Fine/compensation	Offenders must pay money, perhaps to the victim
Fixed Penalty Notice (FPN)	On-the-spot fines issued by the police for low-level crimes such as littering
Supervised Attendance Order (SAO)	Alternative to prison for those who cannot pay fines
Probation	Supervision for 6 months to 3 years, which may be combined with rehabilitation programmes
Community Service Order (CSO)	Requirement to carry out up to 300 hours of unpaid work in the community
Restriction of Liberty Order (RLO; electronic tagging)	Offenders are given a curfew and their movements are restricted for 12 hours a day. Offenders must wear a transmitter that alerts the police if they violate their agreed conditions
Drug Treatment and Testing Order (DTTO)	This is a rehabilitation-based sentence during which people are subjected to random drug testing and court reviews to monitor their withdrawal from drugs
Home detention curfew	Offenders must be in an agreed address by a certain time each day and if the curfew is broken they may be sent to prison
Community Reparation Order (CRO)	Offenders must complete up to 100 hours of unpaid work in the community
Antisocial Behaviour Order (ASBO)	This bans someone (over the age of 12) from causing disruption with their behaviour. ASBOs can be issued for crimes such as graffiti, noise pollution and littering. They are also used to try to keep people away from certain areas. Broken ASBOs can lead to fines or up to 5 years in prison.

Proposals for change

- More Supervised Bail Orders, reducing the number of people in jail before trial.
- More conditional sentences, with prison sentences imposed for not meeting conditions.
- Introduction of progress courts reviewing people on community sentences.

THINGS TO DO AND THINK ABOUT

1   Class debate: 'The not proven verdict should be abolished in Scotland.'

2   More non-custodial sentencing should be introduced in Scotland instead of prison.

   Do you agree or disagree with this statement? Explain your answer. Use the 'Rethinking crime and punishment' online link.

THE SCOTTISH JUVENILE JUSTICE SYSTEM

YOUTH CRIME IN SCOTLAND

There were 1095 crimes among under-10s reported to police in 2011–12. Over 3200 crimes, including knife carrying, assault and sexual exposure, are alleged to have been committed by children under 10 in the past 3 years.

Strathclyde had the highest rate of reporting for child offending in Scotland in 2011-12, with police responding to 212 incidents. Two 8-year-olds were found carrying knives and two 9-year-olds were reported for a sexual assault on a girl in the region. Other alleged crimes include instances of breach of the peace, vandalism and racially aggravated conduct.

Under Scots law, children under the age of 8 are not held criminally responsible for their actions but can be referred to the Children's Hearing System on welfare grounds. Children between the ages of 9 and 12 can be dealt with for offending at children's hearings, while only those aged 12 and over can be prosecuted in court, if the offence is considered serious enough.

VIDEO LINK

Watch the 'Knife crime' animation for more on youth knife crime in Scotland: www.brightredbooks.net/ N5ModernStudies.

THE CHILDREN'S REPORTER

Scotland has its own justice system when dealing with people under 16 (and occasionally under 18). The system was implemented on the recommendation of the Kilbrandon Report and is part of the Children (Scotland) Act 1995. The Procurator Fiscal decides whether or not to prosecute and may refer children to the Children's Reporter.

The Children's Reporter receives referrals regarding children and decides if action is required. Referrals can be made by the police, social workers, health and education professionals, members of the public and even the children themselves. Offence referrals to the Children's Reporter have fallen by 66% since 2006–07.

The Children's Reporter can arrange a hearing if they feel it may be necessary to introduce measures to support the child.

VIDEO LINK

Watch the clip about the scheme credited with reducing youth crime in Dundee for more: www. brightredbooks.net/ N5ModernStudies.

ONLINE

Find out more about the Scottish Children's Reporter online; www.brightredbooks. net/N5ModernStudies.

THE CHILDREN'S HEARING SYSTEM

The Children's Hearing System was introduced in 1971. Hearings are intended to support the child in an informal environment they feel comfortable in and they try to deal with the root causes of any problems. Hearings target both offending behaviour and welfare concerns, and aim to provide a safe environment for the child to discuss issues and problems.

The child is present at every meeting and they can bring a person of their choosing as well as their parents or guardians. Parents or guardians may be fined if they do not attend hearings, but in some cases they may be asked to leave the room if it makes the child more comfortable.

Meetings take place in the child's local area with three adult children's hearing members present. The panel must be made up of both men and women, and there are around 2500 people across Scotland who volunteer for this role. They are impartial and fully trained. Every Scottish local authority has a children's hearing panel.

A child may be placed before a hearing if they:

- are beyond the control of their parents or guardians
- are at risk of moral danger

- are the victim of an offence
- are likely to suffer serious harm
- are misusing drugs and/or alcohol or solvents
- have committed an offence
- are not attending school regularly without a reasonable excuse
- are subject to an ASBO.

What can hearings recommend?

The children's hearing panel can recommend discharging the referral because they feel that no action is needed. However, if action is required the panel can recommend that the child should be put under a compulsory supervision order (CSO). In most cases, the child will stay in their home and be placed under the supervision of a social worker who will be allocated specifically to them, but if a CSO is recommended, the child may be placed in care. This may mean they move in with relatives or foster carers, or into a children's home or secure accommodation. A CSO may limit who the child can associate with and force them into a rehabilitation or behaviour programme. Children's hearings can also restrict the movements of a child by issuing them with an electronic tag.

These requirements are reviewed at another hearing within a year. If a child or their family wish to appeal a decision made by a panel they can do so via the Sheriff Court within 21 days. A panel may also refer a case to the Sheriff Court if they are unsure how to proceed.

Strengths and criticisms of children's hearings

Strengths	Criticisms
More appropriate surroundings for young people	Slow to implement change
Children are active participants	Shortage of resources

Polmont Young Offenders' Institution.

YOUNG OFFENDERS

Young people can be sent to a young offenders' institution if they have been found guilty of crimes or whilst they are on **remand** and awaiting trial.

Prisoners take part in activities that educate, develop skills and personal qualities, and prepare them for life outside prison. They are also encouraged to exercise regularly.

Young offenders can undertake educational courses and gain qualifications in trades such as bricklaying and joinery. There is also a range of rehabilitation programmes and courses such as the Violence Prevention Programme (VPP).

Polmont Young Offenders' Institution (YOI) near Falkirk is Scotland's national holding facility for young male offenders aged between 16 and 21 years of age. Sentences range from 6 months to life and the average sentence length is between 2 and 4 years.

HMP (Her Majesty's Prison) Cornton Vale in Stirling houses female young offenders in Scotland.

THINGS TO DO AND THINK ABOUT

1 Why should a children's panel be made up of both men and women?

2 Why do you think the system was introduced?

3 Role-play how a children's hearing would be carried out.

 DON'T FORGET

The Children and Young People (Scotland) Bill was introduced in 2013 and may result in changes to the justice system.

 FACT

The reconviction rate for young offenders under the age of 21 was 36.1% in 2009-10 compared to 42.4% in 1997-98.

 ONLINE TEST

Test your knowledge by taking the 'The Scottish juvenile justice system' test at www.brightredbooks.net/N5ModernStudies.

SOURCE-BASED QUESTIONS: DECISION MAKING

These questions require you to use sources to make a decision about a given Social Issues topic. There is no right or wrong answer as you are only required to justify the decision you make. You will be given two options to choose from and must provide at least one reason why you rejected the other option.

Take the time to read the question carefully and analyse the sources before you make your decision. You must refer to all the sources provided at least once in your answer and you should show interaction between the sources, matching up written and statistical sources.

SAMPLE DECISION MAKING QUESTION

Study Sources 1, 2 and 3, then answer the question which follows.

You are an adviser to the Government. You have been asked to recommend whether the Government should increase the state pension age to 68 years.

SOURCE 1

Option 1	Option 2
The Government should increase the state pension age to 68 years.	The Government should not increase the state pension age to 68 years.

Facts and Viewpoints

The Government is considering increasing the age at which people can receive the state pension from 65 to 68 years.

- Life expectancy has risen considerably since pensions were first introduced; more people are living longer and claiming pensions for longer.

- The UK Government spent just over £122 billion on pensions in 2011; each year this figure continues to rise.

- If the pension age is increased to 68 years, approximately 2.6 million women and 2.3 million men in the UK will have to wait longer than expected to receive their state pension.

- There is a gap in life expectancy between men and women.

- Many believe that if people work longer it will help the economy as they will still be paying tax on their income and not claiming a pension.

- Due to the economic crisis, the Government needs to reduce its debt, which was over £900 billion in 2011.

- The National Audit Office estimated that £1.162 trillion was spent on bailing out the banks at various points between 2007 and 2011.

- Forcing people to work longer will mean fewer opportunities for young people getting into work.

SOURCE 2

Current pension age and planned pension age in selected European countries.

Country	Current Pension Age (years)	Planned Pension Age (years)
France	60	62
Germany	65	67
Italy	60	65
Greece	65 (male) 60 (female)	65 (all)
Austria	65 (male) 62 (female)	No change
Netherlands	65	66
UK	65	68

Survey Question: Do you agree with the Government's plans to increase the state pension age to 68 years for both men and women?

Yes	49%
No	40%
Don't Know	11%

SOURCE 3

Viewpoints

Giving people the opportunity to work longer is a positive step. Having a few extra years to add to your pension fund means a more financially secure retirement. It is unrealistic for anyone to expect that after working for 30-35 years the Government should then finance a 25-30 year retirement. Every year the amount of money paid out in pensions by the Government continues to rise. The Government simply cannot afford to continue paying out more money given the current financial situation. Every other European country is having to increase its pension age. Many workers have in the past been forced to retire against their will. Most people at 65 years would be happy to work for another few years.

Ross Dale

Increasing the age of retirement will be a disaster. When I started working I expected to work until I was 60 years old. As a woman I have already had to accept that I must work another five years and now the Government want to increase this further. People in Britain already work longer than many other European countries. I fear that I will actually work until the day I die. It is even worse for men who tend not to live as long as women. It is not possible for workers in some jobs to carry on until they are 68 years old. It is unfair to force people to carry on working in these jobs. Why should hardworking people be forced to pay for the economic crisis caused by the banks?

Mary Birch

You must decide which option to recommend, **either** increase the state pension age to 68 (**Option 1**) or not increase the state pension age to 68 (**Option 2**).

(i)   Using Sources 1, 2 and 3, state which option you would choose.
(ii) Give reasons to support your choice.
(iii) Explain why you did not choose the other option.
Your answer must be based on all three sources.

8 marks

HOW TO LAY OUT YOUR ANSWER

DON'T FORGET

Decision making questions will be assessed in the Social Issues unit of the course but may refer to any topic you have studied in the final exam.

Start by stating the option you have chosen. *(Outcome 1.1: Making a decision using between two and four sources of information.)*

> I have chosen Option 1; the Government should increase the state pension age to 68.

Justify your decision. You should provide reasons using evidence from the sources. *(Outcome 1.2: Justifying, in detail, a decision based on evidence from between two and four sources of information.)*

> One reason I chose Option 1 is because **Source 1** clearly states life expectancy has risen considerably since pensions were first introduced; more people are living longer and claiming pensions for longer. This is supported by **Source 2** which shows that Scottish life expectancy has increased significantly between 2000 and 2008 for both males and females. In 2000, female life expectancy was approximately 79 years and by 2008 this had increased to approximately 80 years. Male life expectancy has increased from approximately 73 years in 2000 to approximately 76 years in 2008.

> Another reason I chose Option 1 is because **Source 2** states that other European countries are planning to increase their state pension age. Germany plans to increase from 65 to 67 and France from 60 to 62. **Source 3** supports this by stating 'every other European country is having to increase its pension age'. The UK is part of the European Union and should try to have similar policies to other European countries.

> A final reason I chose Option 1 is because **Source 3** states that 'most people at 65 would be happy to work for another few years'. This is supported in **Source 1** which states that 'many people believe that if they work longer it will help the economy as they will still be paying tax on their income and not claiming a pension'. Therefore many British people would be happy to work longer and increase the state pension age to 68.

Using the Sources clearly state why you rejected the other Option. *(Outcome 1.3: Showing an awareness of alternative views.)*

> I did not choose Option 2 (do not increase the pension age) as although in **Source 3** Mary Birch says 'why should hardworking people be forced to pay for the economic crisis caused by the banks', **Source 1** states that due to the economic crisis, the Government needs to reduce its spending and debt, which was over £900 billion in 2011 and **Source 2** shows that 49% of people asked if they agreed with the Government's plans to increase the state pension age to 68 said yes which was the highest figure. 40% said no and 11% said they didn't know.

INTERNATIONAL ISSUES

INTERNATIONAL ISSUES: AN OVERVIEW

In this unit we will be learning about different countries and international issues. These countries and issues are linked to Scotland and have an impact on our lives.

WORLD POWERS

This topic will investigate three countries: Brazil (pages 86–91), India (pages 92–97) and the USA (pages 96–101). We will look into the political system of each of these countries, and the social and economic issues that exist there.

We should learn about these countries because of their international influence.

The USA is the wealthiest country in the world and is home to countless companies that operate in many countries, including the UK, for example Apple and Nike. Although Brazil and India are not as powerful as the USA they have been identified as growing countries that are becoming more powerful. As a result of their rapidly expanding economies and increasing participation in international issues they are part of the **BRICS** nations.

We should also learn about these countries because they are linked to the UK through international organisations such as the G20, the UN and NATO. Through these organisations these countries work with each other to tackle international issues.

G20

The Group of Twenty (**G20**) is an international alliance of 19 countries and the European Union (EU) that was created in 1999. They work together to devise strategies to improve the world's economy and aim to make it as stable as possible. These countries are very powerful, for example combined they account for 90% of global GDP and 80% of international trade. They are also home to two-thirds of the world's population.

Members: Argentina, Australia, Brazil, Canada, China, the EU, France, Germany, India, Indonesia, Italy, Japan, Mexico, Republic of Korea, Russia, Saudi Arabia, South Africa, Turkey, the United Kingdom and the USA.

UN

The UN is an international organisation dedicated to promoting security, social progress and human rights throughout the world. There are currently 193 UN members, who are working toward a range of goals and aims to improve the lives of millions of people. The USA, like the UK, has a permanent seat on the UN Security Council. This position allows them to veto international action discussed by the UN.

NATO

The North Atlantic Treaty Organisation (NATO) is made up of 28 countries that work together to ensure peace and security. The organisation has been involved in many international conflicts, including the wars in Bosnia and Afghanistan.

Members: Albania, Belgium, Bulgaria, Canada, Croatia, Czech Republic, Denmark, Estonia, France, Germany, Greece, Hungary, Iceland, Italy, Latvia, Lithuania, Luxembourg, the Netherlands, Norway, Poland, Portugal, Romania, Slovakia, Slovenia, Spain, Turkey, the UK and the USA.

WORLD ISSUES

In this topic we are going to explore three international issues: **human rights** (pages 104–109), child soldiers (pages 110–113) and international inequalities (pages 114–119). We will examine the cause and impacts of each of the issues and assess the attempts to resolve them.

Human rights

Not all countries have the same level of human rights that we do here in the UK. The UK is committed to promoting and defending human rights across the world. Being part of international organisations such as the UN and international pressure groups, and supporting local campaigns achieve this.

By using Libya as a case study we can discover the ways in which the international community can intervene when human rights are being denied by a government on a national scale.

The international pressure group Amnesty International is an example of how charity organisations can actively promote and improve human rights. We will look at the use of the death penalty as an example of this.

Local people are also able to make a difference in individual human rights cases. By exploring women's rights in Afghanistan we can compare life in Afghanistan to life in the UK and discover the ways that people are trying to change their own situation. We will also study the case of Pussy Riot in Russia, where the government is accused of not permitting as much freedom of expression as we experience in the UK.

Child soldiers

As part of the international community that condemns the use of children in war the UK is part of resolutions to stop child soldiers. The UK's army and non-government groups are also restricted by international law as to who can fill their ranks. Without these laws life for children in Scotland could be very different.

This section outlines the laws in place to protect children and the problems that exist with regard to these laws. We will then go on to learn about what life is like for children who become soldiers and what action has been taken to help them.

International inequality

Not everyone has access to basic requirements such as food, health care or education. These are aspects of life that here in the UK we can take for granted. The international community has acknowledged these inequalities and has made a commitment to work together to reduce them.

As part of this commitment eight **Millennium Development Goals** were created:

1 Eradicate extreme poverty and hunger.

2 Achieve universal primary education.

3 Promote gender equality and empower women.

4 Reduce child mortality.

5 Improve maternal health.

6 Combat HIV/AIDS, malaria and other diseases.

7 Ensure environmental sustainability.

8 Set up global partnership of development.

The UK is part of the group working towards achieving these goals. We will study three of the areas: world hunger, education and child mortality.

WORLD POWER: BRAZIL

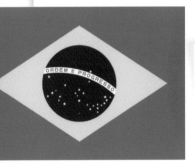

BRAZIL'S POLITICAL SYSTEM

In Brazil there is one government that has authority over the whole country and separate states with specific powers, this is known as a federal government. The current constitution was created in 1988 and was the country's turning point from military dictatorship to a democratic system of government. Since its creation it has had over 30 amendments.

FEDERAL GOVERNMENT: EXECUTIVE BRANCH (THE UNION)

The executive branch of the Brazilian government is made up of a Cabinet of ministers for each executive area and is headed by the president and the vice-president. In 2010 Brazil gained its first female president: Dilma Rousseff. Women are historically under-represented in the Cabinet, but Rousseff's Cabinet contains a record number of female ministers (10, 26%).

To become president the candidate has to win an outright majority in the first set of elections. If this is not achieved then the first and second candidates must have a run-off election to determine the winner.

PROFILE: DILMA ROUSSEFF (36TH PRESIDENT)

Born	1947
Party	Workers' Party
Previous positions	Energy Minister (2003), Chief of Staff (2005)
Background	Supported an underground resistance to the 1964 military dictatorship, resulting in her being jailed for 3 years
Education	Economics
Powers	• Outlined in Article 21 of the Constitution • Command armed forces • Appoint commanders of the forces • Appoint a range of senior officials, including the Supreme Court Ministers and the President of the Central Bank (Note: These appointments have to be approved by Congress) • With approval of Congress, declare war • Plan the budget • Veto laws suggested by Congress • Propose laws to Congress

PRESIDENTIAL ELECTIONS 2010

Brazil's government has a history of corruption. In 2010 Rousseff was involved in issues of corruption when her right-hand woman and Chief of Staff, Erenice Guerra, was forced to step down after it was revealed that government contracts had been given to her son's company.

Election results

First round

Dilma Rousseff (Workers' Party): 46.91% (47,651,434)
Jose` Serra (Social Democratic Party): 32.61% (33,132,283)
Marina Silva (Green Party) 19.33%: (19,636,359)

Second round

Dilma Rousseff: 56.05% (55,752,529)
Jose` Serra: 43.95% (43,711,388)

FEDERAL GOVERNMENT: LEGISLATIVE BRANCH

The National Congress is the legislative branch of the Brazilian Government and contains two houses: the Chamber of Deputies and the Federal Senate.

House	Seats	Voting system	Term
Chamber of Deputies	513 Each state and the federal district have representatives based on the size of its population Minimum of eight and maximum of 70 deputies allowed per state	List system (proportional representation)	4 years
Federal Senate	81 Three per state and the federal district	FPTP	8 years

It is the National Congress's role to pass new laws, and both the Chamber and the Senate must pass every law. They also have the power to authorise the president to declare war.

JUDICIAL BRANCH

The role of the judicial branch is to protect the rights of citizens and ensure the constitution is upheld. The Supreme Federal Court is the highest court in Brazil and comprises 11 ministers that are chosen by the president and approved by the Senate. Cases can be appealed to the Supreme Federal Court from the lower courts and as a result the court has an extensive workload: in 2008 it dealt with 100,781 cases!

STATE GOVERNMENT

There are 26 states and one federal district, where the capital, Brasilia, is located. Each state has its own government and set of powers. Any power that is not enshrined in federal law belongs to the states. The governor and legislative assembly in each state have power over local state issues such as policing and the criminal justice system. They also work with the federal government to provide health and education. Elections are held every 4 years.

MUNICIPALITIES

Brazil is divided further into over 5500 separate municipalities that deal with local council issues. Each area covers on average 35,000 residents and states have around 214 municipalities each. The municipalities can pass laws on local issues and are headed by an elected mayor.

ELECTRONIC VOTING

Electronic voting was first introduced in Brazil in 1996. It didn't take long to develop and by 2000 all votes were cast this way. The government claims that this makes the process easier for citizens and reduces the number of mistakes. Each candidate is allocated a number and voters select their choice. The computer also shows the picture of each of the candidates to ensure they are making the correct numerical selection. It takes just 6 hours to count the votes!

PRESSURE GROUPS

Landless Workers' Movement

- 1.5 million members in 23 of 27 states.
- Campaigns for the distribution of unused land.
- Built farms, houses and schools on the land they have gained.

Central Unica dos Trabalhadores

- Highly influential trade union.
- Represents over 7.4 million workers.
- Campaigns to improve the rights of workers.

FACT

Voting is compulsory for citizens aged between 18 and 70.

FACT

If the president or vice-president wish to leave Brazil for more than 15 days they have to gain permission from the National Congress.

DON'T FORGET

You should use Brazilian examples in your answers.

ONLINE

Check out the Brazilian government website for research at www.brightredbooks.net/N5ModernStudies.

ONLINE TEST

Take the 'Brazil's political system' test online at www.brightredbooks.net/N5ModernStudies.

THINGS TO DO AND THINK ABOUT

1. Create a diagram showing the structure of Brazil's political system.
2. What problem is there within Brazilian politics? Has this ever happened in the UK?
3. Does Brazil use any voting systems that are used in the UK?
4. In what ways can Brazilian citizens participate in politics?

INEQUALITIES IN BRAZIL: DRUGS AND POVERTY

BRAZIL'S DRUG PROBLEM

Recent studies have revealed that there are around 1–1.2 million crack users in Brazil, making it the second largest consumer of cocaine in the world. Brazil has had problems with cocaine since the 1990s, but recently there has been an increase in demand for both powder cocaine and crack.

Traffickers pay $50/kg and cocaine is shipped to Porto Velho for $250/kg, then sold for $6000/kg in Sao Paulo.

The previous president, President Lula, took a different approach to drug abuse and viewed the issue as a health problem. As a result he changed the law and people who possess or use drugs are no longer arrested or imprisoned. Instead they are issued with fines or put on community service and/or treatment programmes. However, it is very difficult to split those who are selling and those who are using the drugs themselves. This means that there are still large numbers of people being imprisoned. There has been so much controversy over the large number of imprisonments that an interest group called Drug Law: It's Time to Change has emerged.

President Dilma Rousseff has also focused on dealing with Brazil's drug problem:

- Border patrols have been increased.
- The number of soldiers policing the border has been increased.
- A $2 billion drug-prevention and treatment programme has been set up.

CITY CASE STUDY: DRUGS IN SAO PAULO

Sao Paulo, the largest city in Brazil, has experienced problems with drugs for a long time. The area where there are large numbers of drug users and dealers has been renamed 'Cracolandia', meaning 'Crackland'. Throughout the past two decades the streets in this area have been inundated with an estimated 2000 users. This has had a devastating impact on the area. Law-abiding citizens have moved away, businesses have to shut early in the evening and rent has become very cheap. Although there is an official population of around 12,000 there are no childcare, education or health systems. Rubbish is also a major factor, with drug users and squatters scavenging for food.

Dor e Sofrimento (Pain and Suffering)

Local authorities have tried to redistribute the street addicts into different areas in order to break up the high population. Authorities discovered that this tactic didn't deal with the long-term problem but just increased the number of areas affected by drugs.

Drug-treatment centres

Some authorities have required addicts to attend drug-treatment centres. A very popular centre called CRATOD is located in Parque da Luz, near Cracolando. Addicts can attend drop-in sessions and receive the support and advice they need. Many people will volunteer to attend these centres, but the drop-out rate is very high on long-term programmes. Although the centres can help there are very few of them and they are overwhelmed by the number of people needing support.

POVERTY IN BRAZIL

- Poverty line: between R$70.01 and R$140 per person per month.

- Extreme poverty line: R$70 or below per person per month.

Brazil is a country of great inequality and there is a vast gap between the rich and the poor. Although there has been an economic boom in recent years, there are still significant levels of inequality. The Workers' Party has made tackling poverty a key issue and both President Lula and President Rousseff have made a positive impact.

When Lula was in power between 2003 and 2011, household income increased by 27%. Unemployment rates also improved, with a decrease from 9.1% in 2002 to 6.8% in 2011. When President Rousseff took over from Lula she made the promise to eliminate extreme poverty in the duration of her term. Studies have shown that the Workers' Party has pulled 28 million people out of extreme poverty since it gained power in 2003. Despite this progress 26% of people were living in poverty in 2012, 16.2 million remained in extreme poverty and 4.8 million people had no income at all.

President Lula

Consolidated the previous government's welfare policies and increased funding:

- 'Bolsa Famila' – part of Lula's 'Fome Zero' initiative to ensure that every Brazilian has enough food to eat.

- Money for mothers who send their children to school.

- A special credit card for buying food.

- Financial support to purchase gas cylinders.

- Consolidated welfare recipient list.

- Funding increase from R$2.4 billion in 2002 to R$8.3 billion in 2006.

President Rousseff

'Extreme poverty in Brazil will soon become extinct.' (Rousseff, 2013.)

'Brasil Sem Miseria' (Brazil Without Misery).

When President Rousseff first came to power in 2011 she added another 2.8 million people to the welfare list and helped an extra 22 million out of extreme poverty by giving them extra cash benefits.

- *Bolsa Familia*: a programme originally for children under the age of 15 to ensure that income per person was R$70, but now extended to include any family receiving social welfare.

- *Busca Ativa* (Active Search): this policy was created to meet the needs of poor people who lived in rural and isolated areas of Brazil. Rousseff believes there are about 2.5 million people who do not receive benefits they are entitled to because they live in isolated areas and lack the required information.

ONLINE

For more on President Lula, read his BBC profile at www.brightredbooks.net/ N5ModernStudies.

DON'T FORGET

Make sure you always explain how the government's policies help meet the needs of people.

ONLINE

For more on President Rousseff, read her BBC profile at www. brightredbooks.net/ N5ModernStudies.

THINGS TO DO AND THINK ABOUT

1 Make a list of all the problems that drug addiction causes. Consider the impact on the local area, families, the individual and the government.

2 What evidence is there to suggest that poverty within Brazil is decreasing?

ONLINE TEST

Take the 'Inequalities in Brazil' test online at www.brightredbooks.net/ N5ModernStudies.

INEQUALITIES IN BRAZIL: HOUSING AND THE RAINFOREST

CASE STUDY: CITY SLUMS

As the population in Brazil's cities has grown so has the problem of inadequate housing. Research carried out in 2013 discovered that São Paulo is the tenth most expensive city in the world to live in, with Rio ranked twelfth. Despite this there is a shortage of 8 million houses, with 50 million people living in poor housing. Over 24 million people in city areas don't have access to drinking water, and 83 million homes do not have an adequate sewage system. Poor areas in the city are known as slums or **favelas**.

Rio

Drug gangs, who have had full control of the slum areas, have dominated the city of Rio. However, the government has made a huge effort to overthrow the drug gangs and take back these areas. Since 2011 the authorities have removed drug gangs from many favelas and regenerated these areas. This process is referred to as 'slum pacification' and was put in place in order to help the city prepare for the 2014 World Cup and 2016 Olympics. As a result of this process crime has decreased, with murder rates dropping, and the areas are now viewed as a great real estate investment.

BRAZIL'S ECONOMY

Brazil is the most powerful South American country and is one of the BRICS nations. The economy is based on the agriculture, mining and service sectors, and is continuing to grow.

Despite the global recession, which took its toll on Brazil, the economy did not collapse and is slowly recovering. Gross Domestic Product (GDP) per person has continued to grow and in 2011 was R$19,000. This has had a positive impact of the levels of poverty within the country and Brazil is predicted to reach its Millennium Development Goal of poverty reduction by 2015.

Farming

Brazil has been very successful with farming for sugar cane, coffee and tropical fruits, and is currently the world's biggest producer of these goods. The value of crops increased from R$23 billion in 1996 to R$108 billion in 2006. Brazil also has 170 million animals, which form the world's biggest commercial cattle herd.

FACT

BRICS nations are the emerging powerful economy countries: Brazil, Russia, India, China and South Africa.

DON'T FORGET

Make sure you stay up to date with the changes happening in Brazil as the country prepares to host the Olympics.

AMAZON RAINFOREST

The Amazon rainforest has been utilised by Brazil and is a key part of the economy. Although the Amazon has generated a lot of wealth for Brazil its use by humans has created several problems.

The Amazon rainforest is spread over nine countries but Brazil has a 60% share of the rainforest and it takes up half of the country. The rainforest is home to thousands of different plants and animals as well as indigenous people. There are over 200 indigenous groups that speak over 120 languages.

FACT

The Amazon rainforest produces over 20% of the world's oxygen.

WHAT IS IT USED FOR AND WHAT IS THE IMPACT?

Through a process of **deforestation** the Amazon rainforest has been cut down to make space for a range of money-making activities. Unfortunately, this deforestation has caused significant long-term problems.

Logging

The Amazon contains trees that can be cut down and sold for building supplies, furniture and charcoal. Hardwoods such as rosewood, mahogany and teak are in large demand from countries worldwide. For example, Japan imports 11 million cubic metres of wood every year.

Trees are also cut down to produce fuel that generates electricity for factories within the Amazon. For example, a steel factory requires millions of tons of wood for fuel each year.

The paper industry is also very significant in Brazil and one plant can produce pulp worth $5000 a day. But large areas of the rainforest have to be cut down to create space to grow pulpwood trees. Roads also have to be built to allow for transport in and out of the plants. For example, one plant in the Amazon has cut down 5600 square miles of rainforest to plant pulpwood trees and uses 2000 tons of wood to create electricity every day.

Grazing land

A large amount of the Amazon has been turned into grazing land for cattle ranches. In order to set up these ranches, trees and surrounding ecosystems have to be destroyed. Cattle ranches have rapidly increased in Brazil; production doubled between 1990 and 2002.

Cattle ranch statistics
220 million cattle
20 million goats
60 million pigs
700 million chickens

Using land for grazing has some devastating consequences:

- 80% of areas that have been torn down are used for grazing land.
- An area the size of Portugal was created for cattle ranching between 1996 and 2006.
- After the land has been used it is severely damaged and it will be years before anything can grow again.

Source of medicine

The Amazon rainforest is home to thousands of plants that are key components of life-saving drugs, but because of deforestation these plants and their homes are being destroyed.

- A quarter of medicines contain ingredients from the rainforest.
- 121 prescription drugs contain plants that can be located only in the rainforest.
- The US National Cancer Institute has discovered there are at least 3000 cancer-fighting plants in the world and 70% grow in the rainforest.

PROTECTING THE RAINFOREST

The Brazilian Government has put many policies in place to protect the rainforest.

Bolsa Floresta: Forest Conservation Allowance Programme

This programme was created in 2007 and aimed to reduce deforestation. After completing a 2-day training course and promising to carry out deforestation families were given a yearly benefit of R$1360. The programme also funded health and education projects in the local community. Sustainable businesses that did not require areas of rainforest to be cut down were also supported, such as fish farming and bee keeping.

Forest Code

This was set up in 1965 and is vital to the protection of the Amazon. The code protects certain areas, called legal reserves, and bans deforestation in certain high-risk areas such as slopes or rivers. More areas of the Amazon are being legally protected. For example, in 2006 a law protecting an area of 15 million hectares (the equivalent of Portugal, Denmark and Switzerland added together) in the state of Para was passed. This was great progress for the Amazon as this state is home to the country's largest timber production, most of which is carried out illegally, and a number of endangered species such as the giant anteater and the black spider monkey.

VIDEO LINK

Check out the clip 'Natural balance – threats to the rainforest' for more on this at www.brightredbooks.net/N5ModernStudies.

ONLINE

Check out the page 'Protecting the Brazilian Amazon' at www.brightredbooks.net/N5ModernStudies.

ONLINE TEST

Take the 'Inequalities in Brazil' test online at www.brightredbooks.net/N5ModernStudies.

THINGS TO DO AND THINK ABOUT

1 What are advantages and disadvantages of using the resources within the Amazon rainforest?

WORLD POWER: INDIA

BACKGROUND

As a result of trade influences in the region India was under British Raj (rule) from 1858 until 1947. India was able to gain its independence because of the work of a man called Mohandas 'Mahatma' Gandhi. Gandhi brought together Muslims and Hindus, and led a peaceful anti-British campaign, which involved techniques such as boycotting British goods and fasting. In 1947 the Indian Independence Act came into place, relinquishing British rule and dividing the area into two separate states: India and Pakistan.

FACT

India is also referred to as Bharat.

ONLINE

Research and create a fact file on Gandhi and his achievements.

FACT

India's electorate is bigger than the EU and USA electorates combined!

POLITICAL SYSTEM

India's political system is a **federal republic** and its structure is outlined in the Constitution, written in 1949. In a federal republic lots of smaller states have power but they are all overseen by one central government.

The Constitution is founded on the following principles:

- Justice
- Liberty
- Equality
- Fraternity

EXECUTIVE BRANCH

Within the executive branch there is a range of positions:

- President
- Vice-President
- Prime Minister
- Council of Ministers

President

The president serves for a 5-year term and leads the executive branch of India's government. It is his/her role to implement the laws passed by the legislative branch. The president is required to carry out the actions recommended to him/her by the government.

If parliament does not believe that the president is able to carry out this position the Lok Sabha can impeach him/her and the Rajya Sabha will investigate.

Powers:
- approve laws
- appoint a range of positions, including the prime minister and chief justice
- Commander-in-Chief of the armed forces
- pardoning powers.

The president is not elected by the people of India but rather by the members of an Electoral College. This Electoral College includes members of the parliament and legislative assemblies of the states and uses the single transferable vote system.

Government: prime minister and the Council of Ministers

The government is made up of the prime minister and the Council of Ministers.

It is the prime minister's job to appoint and head the Council of Ministers, and together they advise and support the president. Although the president appoints the prime minister he/she is normally the leader of the majority party in parliament.

DON'T FORGET

The president does not have unlimited power and must work with the other branches of government.

LEGISLATIVE BRANCH

The parliament, which consists of two houses, forms the law-making branch of government. The two houses of the Indian parliament are:

contd

- Council of State – Rajya Sabha
- House of the People – Lok Sabha.

Rajya Sabha

- Maximum 250 members.
- 238 from the 28 states and the 7 union territories.
- 12 nominated by the president and the rest elected by the people of India.
- 6-year term.
- Vice-president is the chairman.

Lok Sabha

- Maximum of 552 members.
- 530 from the states and 20 from the union territories.
- The president can nominate two from the Anglo-Indian community.
- 5-year term.
- All elected by the people of India.

The main role of the parliament is to make laws, and every new law has to be agreed on by both houses. The laws focus on issues that affect the whole of India, such as defence, currency, foreign affairs, customs and communications.

This system of government requires all branches to work together. For example the Lok Sabha will monitor the prime minister and the Council of Ministers, and if they doubt that they are fulfilling their role to the required standard a vote of confidence can be issued, causing the ministers to step down. The president's power is limited because if the Lok Sabha support the prime minister's decision the president cannot go against their action.

GENERAL ELECTIONS 2009

In 2009, 714 million people were eligible to vote in India's general election. This enormous electorate makes India the largest democracy in the world. There were 828,804 polling stations, 1,368,430 electronic voting machines, candidates from 1055 political parties and 543 seats available. Because of the extensive size of the electorate, voting took place between 16 April and 13 May in five phases.

The previous prime minister, Manmohan Singh, and his party the Indian National Congress were re-elected to serve for another 5 years.

The two main parties are the Indian National Congress and the Bharatiya Janata. However, it is very difficult for one party to gain enough seats to become a majority government and as a result several parties have formed coalitions under a number of names:

- United Progressive Alliance
- National Democractic Alliance
- Third Front
- Fourth Front.

JUDICIAL BRANCH

The most powerful court in India is called the Supreme Court and it is located in New Delhi.

The court deals with:

- disputes between government and state
- disputes between the states
- appeals from smaller courts.

There are 25 judges and one chief justice who are appointed by the president until they retire at the age of 65. They must ensure that the Constitution is upheld at all times.

STATES AND UNION TERRITORIES

India contains 28 states and 7 union territories. State government is structured in the same way as the national government. Each state has a governor who works with the chief minister and a Council of Ministers to deal with state issues.

THINGS TO DO AND THINK ABOUT

Make a diagram showing the different branches of the federal government in India.

FACT

Manmohan Singh was the second prime minster to ever be re-elected.

ONLINE

Head to the BrightRED Digital Zone to see the results for the two main coalitions in 2009.

ONLINE TEST

Take the test on India's political system online at www.brightredbooks.net/N5ModernStudies.

ONLINE

For more about the Indian Government take a look at their website at www.brightredbooks.net/N5ModernStudies

INEQUALITIES IN INDIA: CASTE AND WEALTH

POPULATION OF INDIA

India's 2011 census revealed that its population is continuing to grow, with a 17% increase since 2001. This is an increase of 181 million people, making the total population 1.21 billion. India has 17% of the world's population and it has been predicted that its population will be larger than China's by 2030.

FACT

The population of India is bigger than those of the USA, Indonesia, Brazil and Pakistan combined!

VIDEO LINK

Check out the 'Caste system explained' clip to learn more at www.brightredbooks.net/N5ModernStudies.

DON'T FORGET

People who are victims of discrimination are often too scared to report it to the police.

ONLINE

Find out more by checking out the Video Volunteers website at www.brightredbooks.net/N5ModernStudies.

VIDEO LINK

Check out the End Untouchability trailer at www.brightredbooks.net/N5ModernStudies.

HINDU CASTE SYSTEM

The Hindu caste system began nearly 3000 years ago when Indian society was separated into different types of work, also known as Varna. Over time this transformed into a rigid caste system. The caste a person belongs to is wholly dependent on birth and moving between the castes is not permitted.

There are four main castes:

- Brahmin
- Kshatriya
- Vaishya
- Shudra.

There is a final group of people who are not part of the caste system and are instead referred to as 'untouchables' or Dalits. This rigid system generated social tension and discrimination between the castes, in particular towards the untouchables. The Indian Constitution now states that caste discrimination is illegal and in 1989 the Scheduled Castes and Scheduled Tribes (Prevention of Atrocities) Act was passed by the government.

Although it is illegal to discriminate against a person based on caste, the Dalits frequently suffer violence and abuse. For example, children are forced to have lunch away from other students at school, and people are not allowed into certain temples, are refused service at shops and have been attacked for walking on certain streets. In 2005 one man's son and daughter-in-law were murdered as a result of them marrying between castes. The suspects were never charged and the case remains unresolved. Charities have reported that, in 2008, 33,000 crimes were recorded against Dalits, but the number is thought to be a lot higher as many crimes go unreported.

Dealing with the issue: Video Volunteers

Video Volunteers is an international organisation that seeks to use media as a tool to reveal poverty, injustice and inequality in India. Volunteers teach and support local people to gather evidence that is often not covered by the national media and campaign for the issue to be dealt with. In 2012 they launched the campaign 'Article 17' to put pressure on the government department responsible for dealing with protecting Dalits (the National Commission for Scheduled Castes). Through videos of Indians sharing their daily experiences of discrimination the group hope that the government will recognise the issue and take more steps to punish those who are responsible.

INDIA'S WEALTH

India's economy

Like Brazil, India is part of the BRIC nations and its economy has grown rapidly over the past 20 years. The country's growth rates for the past 10 years are between 7% and 9%. In 2010 India's economy had the world's highest growth rate. The number of wealthy people in India is also growing. For example, according to Forbes magazine, in the 1990s there were just two billionaires living in India, with a total fortune of $3.2 billion. By 2012 this had increased to 46 with $176.3 billion.

contd

Wealth and income inequalities

Despite this progression there are vast wealth inequalities across the country. The distribution of India's wealth and success is not equal. The top 10% who earn the highest wages make almost 12 times more than the bottom 10%, which is the largest difference in all evolving economies.

Living in the slums

Across India there are 13.8 million households (64 million people) living in slums that have been classed as unsuitable. These homes often lack sanitation and electricity, and are very poorly built. For example a third of slum homes do not have an inside toilet and 64% do not have a working sewage system. Although slums can be found across the country some areas have more than others.

Percentages of households that live in slums:

- Kolkata: 30%
- Chennai: 29%
- New Delhi: 15%
- Bangalore: 9%

Profile: Mumbai

- Financial capital of India.
- Largest city, with a population of 19 million.
- 1 in 6 people lives in the slums.
- 40% of households live in shanty towns.

With regards to income levels India is becoming increasingly unequal. The ideal official measure of income inequality is 0, but India's levels have increased from 0.32 to 0.38 over the last 20 years. According to an investigation carried out by the Organisation for Economic Co-operation and Development (OECD) India has the highest number of poor people in the world, with 42% of the population surviving on less than $1.25 a day. Places such as Orissa, Chhattisgarh and Bihar in rural areas of central and eastern India are suffering the most.

Rural areas rely on farming to make a living, and 65% of the population are involved in agriculture. However, farmers often struggle to produce enough food to eat or sell, and live in poverty. A farming household will make, on average, 1800 Indian rupees a year.

Government support

Policy	Description
National Rural Employment Guarantee Act 2005	This policy gave all Indians living in rural areas the right to 100 days of paid work within 15 days of asking for it, and within 3 miles of their village
Public Distribution System	Shops have been set up to allocate funded food and other items to poor people across India

CASE STUDY: FAMERS IN BIHAR

Bihar is one the poorest states in India, with about 79% of the population living below the poverty line. Within Bihar farming is the main source of income; 75% of workers are employed in farming. State government, in partnership with the World Bank, has set up a project called the System of Crop Intensification. This project encourages farming methods that have been used across the world to improve farming output. The methods include seed treatment and planting without the use of chemical fertilisers or herbicides. Between 5 and 6 million farmers in China, Indonesia, Cambodia, Sri Lanka and Vietnam have increased their profits using this method. Around 103,000 farmers across the state have successfully followed the project, increasing their crop production and therefore their food supply and income. One farmer doubled his annual income to 100,000 rupees.

THINGS TO DO AND THINK ABOUT

1. Describe what daily life might be like for a Dalit.
2. What evidence is there to suggest that India is a wealthy country?

FACT

It has been reported that only 3% of Indians actually pay tax.

VIDEO LINK

Watch the clip about the squalid conditions in Mumbai's slums to learn more at www.brightredbooks.net/N5ModernStudies.

FACT

More than 50% of the population is below the age of 25.

ONLINE TEST

Take the test on Inequalities in India online at www.brightredbooks.net/N5ModernStudies.

INEQUALITIES IN INDIA: WOMEN'S RIGHTS

WOMEN IN INDIA

Men and women are not equal within India. Women are viewed as the lesser sex and as a result have faced years of discrimination. They are seen as a burden to their families and their personal freedom is heavily restricted.

This preference for males has led to thousands of sex-selective abortions and a high number of child killings. Although these actions are illegal doctors are often bribed to tell the families the sex of a baby before it is born. Fewer and fewer girls are being born or surviving every year. The 2011 census discovered that India still prefers boys over girls, with the gap between boys and girls being higher than ever before. In 2001 there were 927 girls for every 1000 boys under 6. By 2011 this widened to 914 for every 1000.

Life for women

A study carried out in 2012 by the Thomson Reuters Foundation revealed that out of the G20 countries India is the worst place for women to live. This is because of its high rates of infanticide, domestic slavery and child marriage.

Violence towards women is common and viewed as acceptable by many Indians. A study carried out by UNICEF discovered that 52% of teenage girls and 57% of boys believe that is acceptable for a husband to beat his wife. Crimes against women in everyday life have increased; between 2010 and 2011 there was an increase of 7% (National Crime Bureau in India).

Dowry payments

In the past when a woman got married her family paid a dowry to her husband and his family. This payment didn't always take the form of cash, it could be gifts such as cars or a new home. As a result of this system many women were abused. To deal with this issue the system was outlawed in the Dowry Prohibition Act (1961). This Act stated that giving or receiving any dowry exceeding 7000 rupees (£90) is illegal. Although the laws are commonly ignored, the police take dowry-related crimes seriously.

Domestic Violence Act 2005

The government passed an Act in 2005 that outlawed a range of domestic abuse against women. Under the Act physical, sexual and economic abuse are prohibited. Women also gained more rights under this Act. These rights include the right to continue living in a house even if she doesn't own it and the right to help and protection from police and health workers.

SUCCESSFUL WOMEN

Despite these challenges women across India are breaking with tradition and taking on important roles within society.

Naina Lal Kidwai

Naina is a very successful Indian businesswoman who has achieved a lot throughout her career. She is the first Indian woman to:
- graduate from Harvard Business School, where she was also the youngest in her class
- be employed by business company Pricewaterhouse Coopers India
- head a foreign bank in India (HSBC).

Sonia Gandhi

Sonia Gandhi is a powerful and influential Indian politician. Born in Italy she married Rajiv Gandhi and moved to India. After her husband was assassinated she was

FACT

70% of homes in slums have a TV and 64% have mobile phones.

ONLINE TEST

Check out Sonia Gandhi's profile in Forbes magazine at www.brightredbooks.net/N5ModernStudies.

contd

reluctant to enter politics, but eventually joined the Indian National Congress in 1997. In 1998 she was elected president of the party and still holds the position. This makes her the longest-serving president of the Congress party in its 128 years. She has also held the position of chairperson of the ruling United Progressive Alliance in Lok Sabha since 2004.

CASE STUDY: DELHI

There are high levels of abuse and oppression of women in northern India, particularly in Delhi. For example, compared to cities of a similar size, Delhi has the highest recorded number of rape cases, with 630 cases being reported in 2012. On average a rape case is reported every 18 hours and crimes of a sexual nature every 14. This issue received international attention after a brutal rape case in 2012.

The incident

A 23-year-old medical student was travelling on a bus in Delhi when she was beaten and raped by six men, including the bus driver. She was in hospital for 13 days before she died of her injuries.

The aftermath

While the young woman was in hospital, the people of India took to the streets demanding change and justice. Large protests were held the day after the rape happened. The police resorted to tear gas to stop protestors marching to the presidential palace.

'We are marching to create awareness among people that women should be respected. Because a woman is a mother, a woman is a sister, she is a wife and she is a daughter.' (National Commission for Women)

Despite their numbers, it took a week for the prime minister to address the case directly on TV. During a broadcast he asked for the protests to stop and made a pledge to make India a safer place.

Government response

Soon after the woman died it was decided that:
- police would patrol Delhi at night
- there would be checks on bus drivers
- buses with tinted windows would no longer be permitted
- information about convicted rapists would be made available to the public
- committees would be set up to investigate the problems.

Verdict:
- the four men guilty of carrying out the rape have been sentenced to death.

VIDEO LINK

Watch the BBC News report on protests following the incident at www.brightredbooks.net/ N5ModernStudies.

DON'T FORGET

Check the news for any new stories highlighting these issues and any progress that has been made.

ONLINE TEST

Take the test on 'Inequalities in India' online at www. brightredbooks.net/ N5ModernStudies.

THINGS TO DO AND THINK ABOUT

1 Create the front page of a newspaper for the day after the young student died. Consider the following points:
   - what life is like for women in India
   - what had happened to the woman
   - how people reacted
   - what changes the government wanted to put in place.

WORLD POWER: UNITED STATES OF AMERICA

JOURNEY THROUGH POLITICS

Like many countries, such as France and Australia, America's political system is outlined in its Constitution. The American Constitution was created in 1787 with the purpose of explaining the different branches of government and the powers they had been granted. It was important that power was not held by just one branch; this is why the powers are separated and divided. All of the branches have to work together under a system of checks and balances. The Constitution can be, and has been, amended. The first set of changes that were made is referred to as the Bill of Rights.

BRANCHES OF AMERICAN GOVERNMENT

The federal government has the power to deal with issues that have an impact on all American states. These issues include:
- currency
- disputes between states
- armed forces
- postal services
- defence
- foreign affairs.

Although there is one government in charge of the whole of America, each of the 50 states has its own government with power over local issues such as:
- education
- punishments
- local taxes
- road provisions.

Both federal and state governments contain three branches: executive, judicial and legislative.

REPRESENTATION IN AMERICAN POLITICS

The executive

The president heads the executive branch of the federal government. He or she must be an American-born citizen and at least 35 years of age. Presidents can only serve two terms of 4 years in office. The powers of the president are outlined in Article 2 of the Constitution.

Chief legislator	Chief diplomat	Chief executive	Commander-in-chief
• Makes recommendations to Congress • Vetoes Bills	• Creates foreign policy and treaties • Represents the USA in foreign relations	• Appoints officials • Supervises the administration of executive department • Ensures laws are followed	• Decides on war strategies during war • Deploys the military in times of disorder

The legislative

The legislative branch is made up of Congress, which contains the Senate and House of Representatives. American citizens can vote for people to represent them in both Houses. The Senate is made up of two representatives from each state, who serve for up to 6 years. In the House of Representatives each state has roughly one representative for every 400,000 citizens, which results in 435 altogether. Together, these two Houses create America's laws.

Supreme Court

American citizens do not vote for the judges of the Supreme Court. Instead, the president nominates judges and they are approved or rejected by Congress. Supreme Court judges represent American citizens as it is their job to ensure that no laws conflict with the Constitution or American citizens' rights.

GETTING INVOLVED

America is a democratic country and therefore political involvement from citizens is crucial. There are many ways in which American people can participate in the political system and voice their views and opinions.

Join a political party

The two main political parties in America are the Democrat Party and the Republican Party. If citizens join a political party, there are many different ways they can contribute:
- during state primaries they can vote for who they think should be the party's candidate for president
- attend party campaign rallies
- hand out leaflets, stickers and badges promoting their party's candidates
- telephone voters to persuade them to vote for their candidate.

Standing as a candidate/voting

To ensure that all branches of government correctly reflect the views of the population, Americans have the right to vote. If they believe they would be successful at representing the public's views they can stand as a candidate themselves. For example:

- local level: mayor
- state level: governor
- federal level: president

Citizens can also vote on specific issues known as Ballot Measures of Propositions. Examples of this include:

- California 2012 death penalty vote
- Maryland 2012 same-sex marriage vote.

Interest groups

Interest groups try to use their influence to persuade the public to put pressure on politicians either to change or not to change the law. If citizens feel strongly about an issue, they can share their views through a group.

BARACK OBAMA

Barack Obama is the 44th President of the United States of America and made history by being the first African American to hold the position. Obama won the election over John McCain with 365 Electoral College votes. While Obama was in office he managed to get several policies passed and brought about a range of changes. His desire to change the American health care system and his open support towards the gay community resulted in mass debate and controversy.

Domestic policies	International conflicts	Equal rights
Affordable care	End of the Iraq war	Lily Ledbetter Act
Wall Street reform	Assassination of Osama Bin Laden, 2011	Disabilities Act
	START treaty with Russia	Hate Crimes Prevention Act
		Ended 'don't ask don't tell'
		Violence Against Women Act

2012 presidential election

This was the first election where social media sites such as Twitter and Facebook had an influential role. The analysis of voting patterns reveals important changes in the population and distribution of support for the two main parties.

Obama won the election with the majority of support coming from women and ethnic minorities. This is significant because these groups are minorities within the voting population. It reveals the power that these groups have in modern politics.

THINGS TO DO AND THINK ABOUT

Make a table comparing the ways American and British citizens can participate in their country's political systems.

DON'T FORGET

It is really important that you have real-life American examples to support your points.

DON'T FORGET

Remember, the American system does not have MPs or MSPs!

ONLINE

Research the ethos behind the three American interest groups illustrated at www.brightredbooks.net/N5ModernStudies.

ONLINE

Visit www.brightredbooks.net/N5ModernStudies for more statistics from the 2012 election.

ONLINE TEST

Test your knowledge of American politics online at www.brightredbooks.net/N5ModernStudies.

UNITED STATES OF AMERICA: IMMIGRATION

IMMIGRATION

The USA is a country founded on immigrants; for years people have travelled from all over the world to pursue the American dream. Ellis Island in New York opened in 1892 and saw 12 million immigrants pass through its doors into America.

Population breakdown

The USA's population is made up of a range of ethnic groups.

Ethnic group	Percentage of population
White	72.4
Hispanic	16.3
Black	12.6
Asian and Pacific Islander	4.8
Native American	0.9

Figures for 2010.

According to information gathered from the 2010–2011 census there are over 50 million legal and illegal immigrants currently living in the USA. Between 2000 and 2010, immigration increased the population by 22.5 million, which is 80% of the total population growth.

ARGUMENTS IN FAVOUR OF IMMIGRATION

History

Immigration is a huge part of American history and millions of immigrants have contributed to the success of the country. Many people argue that it would be unfair to shut the doors when so many immigrants have enriched America.

Culture

The American population is often referred to as a 'melting pot'. This is the idea that many different races and traditions have joined together to form the American population. This mix means that America has a diverse and varied culture, and is an interesting place to live.

Economy

There is a common stereotype that immigrants take jobs from American citizens or do not contribute to the economy in any way, but this is not true. Many immigrants fill job shortages in America, particularly in the Southern states, and are willing to do low-skilled and low-paid jobs that American citizens do not want to do.

ARGUMENTS AGAINST IMMIGRATION

Social problems

Immigrants can decide not to embrace American culture or tradition, but rather create their own separate areas in towns and cities. For example, 78% of immigrant school children speak English as a second language. As immigrants are willing to work for lower amounts of money this drives down wages and makes it harder for USA citizens to find well-paid jobs, which can also create tensions.

DON'T FORGET

The American dream is the belief that if you work hard there are many opportunities to become successful within the USA.

VIDEO LINK

Hear more about the American dream by watching the video at www.brightredbooks.net/N5ModernStudies.

DON'T FORGET

Historically, the black population has been the largest minority group. However in recent years the Hispanic population has overtaken them and become the largest ethnic group.

FACT

In 2012 the population of the USA was an estimated 313,914,040.

FACT

Between 2000 and 2010, 4 million people from Mexico moved to the USA.

VIDEO LINK

Check out the 'Immigration to the USA' clip to learn more at www.brightredbooks.net/N5ModernStudies.

contd

Crime

Many people are smuggled into America, therefore are living there illegally. Some citizens think this is unfair because they are getting the benefits of living in the country without contributing in ways such as paying tax. Illegal immigrants are also more likely to be involved in organised crimes such as drug dealing.

Cost to taxpayers

Immigrants are much more likely to receive welfare and be supported by the government. For example in 2010 36% of immigrant households received at least one government benefit compared to 23% of native households. This angers citizens as they feel their tax money is being spent supporting immigrants.

ONLINE

Learn more about the American Government's immigration policies at www.brightredbooks.net/N5ModernStudies.

BARACK OBAMA

Obama's focus has been on dealing with the number of illegal immigrants, which is an estimated 11 million. He aims to get as many illegal immigrants into the system as possible to ensure they are paying tax, being subjected to background checks and learning English. To deal with immigration he has four key aims.

Aim	Description	Progress
Increase border control	Reduce the number of people illegally crossing the border into America	The number of people patrolling the border doubled from 10,000 in 2004 to 21,000 in 2011 For the first time the south-west border, between California and Texas, has aerial surveillance
Monitor businesses	Ensure companies only employ legal immigrants	From 2009 the number of companies involved in e-verification has doubled and is now 416,000
Improve the citizenship system	Make it possible for illegal immigrants to gain citizenship	A way of streamlining the system is being developed
Streamline the system	Make it simpler for people to work and study in America	The time families have to spend apart has been reduced

IMMIGRATION AND PRESSURE GROUPS

National protest: 'A Day Without Immigrants' 2006

A reform that meant no illegal immigrant could receive USA citizenship and defined illegal immigration as a crime sparked protest across America. In May 2006 over a million immigrants took part in a nationwide protest to highlight their economic value; they didn't attend school or work and didn't spend any money. President Bush proposed a Guest Worker Programme, which would allow people to work in the USA on a temporary basis to fill jobs that Americans would not do.

State protest: Arizona protests 2010

In 2010 Arizona passed a law that allowed police to question people over their citizenship if they thought they were living in the USA illegally. It also forced immigrants to have their registration papers with them at all times and prohibited illegal immigrants from working. However, many people felt that the law would result in discrimination, with minority groups, particularly Hispanics, being targeted more often. In response to this hundreds of people protested to overturn the law. In 2012 the US Supreme Court stated that Arizona could only enforce the aspect of the law that allowed police to question individuals' legal status.

VIDEO LINK

Check out this CBS News clip about the protest at www.brightredbooks.net/N5ModernStudies.

ONLINE

Read more about 'A Day Without Immigrants' at www.brightredbooks.net/N5ModernStudies.

ONLINE TEST

Test your knowledge of immigration in the USA online at www.brightredbooks.net/N5ModernStudies.

THINGS TO DO AND THINK ABOUT

1 Why might a person want to leave a country and choose to live in America?

2 Create a poster that highlights Obama's immigration goals and the progress he has made.

UNITED STATES OF AMERICA: INEQUALITIES

In this section we are going to investigate whether or not every American has the same chances to succeed.

HEALTH

Country	Life expectancy	Infant mortality per 1000 live births
USA	78.1 years	6.7
UK	79.1 years	4.8
France	81 years	3.8
Singapore	79.7 years	2.1

Health inequalities can be split into two areas:
- level of health
- access to health care.

LEVEL OF HEALTH

Minorities suffer poorer health than whites, particularly the black population. From birth, blacks and Hispanics are more likely to suffer poor health. They have higher rates of obesity, heart disease and HIV/AIDS. These groups are also more likely to have a substance abuse problem. Whites will attend check-ups and health screenings, and therefore are able to identify any health problems early on. This is not the case with blacks and Hispanics. Having poorer health has a life-long impact, leading to further problems later in life.

ACCESS TO HEALTH CARE

Within the USA health care is not funded by the government, instead it is a private system and citizens have to pay for it themselves. They do this through health insurance, which they fund themselves or have provided as part of their job. However, an estimated 45.7 million people do not have health insurance, with minority groups having the highest percentage of people without health insurance.

Even when citizens have health insurance they are often denied treatment or given a limit to the amount of treatment they are allowed to receive.

There are government benefits available: Medicaid and Medicare. Medicaid is for people who have a low income or have additional needs, such as a disability. Medicare is for people 65 years old and over. Although these benefits are available, they don't always cover the treatments required, hospitals are understaffed and don't always have the same access to resources or technology.

Affordable Care Act

This Act has been nicknamed 'Obamacare' and is a range of health reforms that were signed by Obama in 2010. The Act:

- prevents children with pre-existing health problems being rejected by health insurance companies
- removes lifetime treatment caps
- funds small businesses to allow them to be able to provide health care to their workers
- increases free preventive care, for example cancer screenings
- discounts a range of prescription drugs used via Medicare.

DON'T FORGET

Asian and Pacific Islanders have the best health and do very well in school.

FACT

Thirteen per cent of black births are under 2500 grams compared to 7% of white births.

FACT

Infant mortality rates are higher for blacks (13 per 1000 births) than for whites (6 per 1000 births).

DON'T FORGET

Many Hispanic people are in the USA illegally and therefore are not able to access health care.

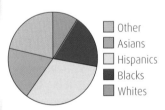

- Other
- Asians
- Hispanics
- Blacks
- Whites

Percentage of people without health insurance.

ONLINE

Check out the breakdown of the US healthcare system at www.brightredbooks.net/N5ModernStudies.

EDUCATION

Dropout rates

Ethnic group	Percentage who drop out of high school
Asian and Pacific Islander	2.1
White	5.2
Black	9.6
Hispanic	17.6

Postcode lottery

There are extensive differences between schools in suburbs and schools located in inner city ghetto areas. Suburban schools are better funded and as a result provide a higher quality of education compared to poorly funded ghetto schools.

Suburban school

- New technology.
- Highly qualified teachers who enjoy teaching there.
- Many sports and extracurricular opportunities.
- Education is highly valued.

Ghetto school

- Run down and old buildings.
- Drug and alcohol issues.
- Limited resources, i.e. textbooks or computers.
- Teachers who don't want to teach there.
- Focus is on a future with gangs rather than further education.

Language barrier

One in four school children in the USA speak English as a second language. For students with very limited English school can be very challenging and they often feel isolated. They may struggle to understand teachers or make friends.

Role models

In ghettos and barrios there is a lack of positive role models to inspire young people. Rather than hoping to move on to further education and have a successful job, young people in ghettos and barrios want to grow up and be part of local gangs.

AFFIRMATIVE ACTION

Some universities have specific race targets and goals to meet and as a result make it easier for minority groups to gain a place over white or Asian candidates. In the past Affirmative Action programmes had a positive impact and appeared to be reducing the education gap. For example, in 1960 5.4% of black people aged 25–29 graduated from college, this had increased to 15.4% in 1995. In addition, the percentage of black law students increased from 1% in 1960 to 7.5% in 1995.

However, in current times many white and Asian students feel that they are being subjected to discrimination when a less-able minority student gains a place instead of them. Groups have campaigned against Affirmative Action programmes and many individuals have taken their cases to court. For example, the University of Michigan had an Affirmative Action scheme that allocated extra admission points to minority groups to boost their chances of meeting the required score. However, in 2003 the Supreme Court declared the scheme to be unconstitutional.

VIDEO LINK

Learn more about the American education system by watching the clip at www.brightredbooks.net/N5ModernStudies.

FACT

60% of black people in the USA that have dropped out of school have served time in prison.

FACT

75% of crimes are committed by high-school dropouts.

FACT

90% of jobs in USA require a high-school education.

ONLINE TEST

Test your knowledge of inequalities in the USA online at www.brightredbooks.net/N5ModernStudies.

THINGS TO DO AND THINK ABOUT

1. When considering health statistics in the USA, the UK, Singapore and France, where would you prefer to live? Give two reasons to support your decision.

2. What challenges do children in the ghetto face when trying to gain an education?

3. Do you think Affirmative Action programmes are a good idea? Give at least three reasons for your answer.

HUMAN RIGHTS

HUMAN RIGHTS IN LIBYA AND THE UNITED NATIONS

Colonel Gaddafi took power in Libya in 1969 after a military coup that overthrew King Idris. At the beginning of his time in power Gaddafi was popular with the people of Libya. However, he was a ruthless dictator who denied his people many of their human rights, which turned the population against him. His extreme and controversial political theories were outlined in his *Green Book*: this was compulsory for Libyans to study and those who disagreed were executed. Colonel Gaddafi also banned all political parties and any opponents were imprisoned, tortured or killed.

A sequence of revolutions, referred to as the **Arab Spring**, started in 2010 and saw the governments of Libya's neighbouring countries of Tunisia and Egypt overthrown by their people. This inspired the population of Libya to rise against Colonel Gaddafi and was the start of bitter conflict that ended in his death in October 2011.

Colonel Gaddafi's strong and heavily armed army responded to the rebels in Tripoli with extreme violence, breaking international law and killing thousands of innocent civilians. The Arab League asked the UN to intervene when Colonel Gaddafi planned to take back the city of Benghazi from the rebels.

VIDEO LINK

Head to the BrightRED Digital Zone and watch the clip about Libya under the rule of Gaddafi.

VIDEO LINK

Check out the video for an explanation of how Gaddafi's power collapsed at www.brightredbooks.net/N5ModernStudies.

United Nations

FACT

The Universal Declaration of Human Rights sets the Guinness World Record for Most Translated Document. It has been translated into 403 different languages.

ONLINE

Using the UN website research different human rights bodies and their specific roles.

DON'T FORGET

Countries have different rights enshrined in law, therefore not every country has the same rights. For example, owning a gun in America is a right protected by law, but this is not the case in the UK.

THE UNITED NATIONS

Set up in 1945 with just 51 members; the UN is an international organisation dedicated to promoting security, social progress and human rights throughout the world. The founding member states created a document known as the Declaration of Human Rights. This document is very important as it outlines and protects the rights of people across the world. Human rights have been enshrined in international law and the member states have made a commitment to develop them within their countries. The UN protects these human rights and can intervene when people are being denied them.

The Office of the High Commissioner for Human Rights is in charge of supporting the UN's Human Rights network. This network is divided into charter-based bodies and treaty-based bodies.

The Human Rights Council is a charter-based body that researches, reports and monitors human rights in countries and specific events of human rights violations. The Council works with the Office of the High Commissioner for Human Rights. The Council meets for 10 weeks a year and has 47 elected UN member states that serve 3-year terms.

RESOLUTIONS

Libya was a member of both the Human Rights Council and a range of international human rights treaties, and therefore should have been promoting and protecting its citizens' rights.

In order to address the increasing problems in Libya the Human Rights Council held a special session in February 2011.

The Human Rights Council was concerned about several issues in Libya at the time:
- extreme violence against peaceful protestors
- banning of the media and telecommunications
- poverty, torture and enforced disappearances
- injured and displaced civilians
- doctors struggling to cope
- imprisonment of lawyers and journalists who were defending human rights.

contd

These attacks on the civilian population had been deemed as crimes against humanity and the Council agreed that the Libyan Government had broken international law. This meant that any government official could be held criminally responsible.

Resolutions:
- release unfairly imprisoned individuals
- cease intimidation, arrests and the tyranny of citizens
- end attacks on the civilian population
- remove the media and telecommunications ban
- set up an independent inquiry to investigate progress

SUPPORTING LIBYA'S TRANSITION

When Gaddafi was killed the new state had the opportunity to rebuild for the first time after 42 years of oppression.

At the core of this new era was the promotion of human rights. In order to support the protection of human rights, the UN set up the United Nations Support Mission in Libya (UNSMIL). This was led by Tarek Mitri and was part of the original resolution.

As well as the UNSMIL there is a range of UN specialised agencies, funds and programmes operating in Libya.

United Nations Children's Fund (UNICEF) 	• Researched into and assessed all 4800 schools • Created the High Council for Childhood, who promote child protection laws, train social workers and improve social protection networks
World Health Organisation (WHO) 	• Support the development of the health care system • Train health workers, for example doctors and nurses
United Nations High Commission For Refugees (UNHCR)	• Support the fundamental needs of refugees • Provision of health clinics, vocational training courses, psycho-social counselling and national legal aid clinics
World Food Programme (WFP)	• Served 2.6 million meals to refugees fleeing to Tunisia and Egypt. • Chartered ships to bring food into Libyan ports – for one million Libyans in need. • Helped rebuild the country by providing training to Libyan officials.
United Nations Development Programme (UNDP)	• Assisted the first democratic elections in 50 years on 7 July 2012 by providing voter education, encouraging the participation of women and giving logistical support.
United Nations Population Fund (UNFPA)	• Promote women's health rights • Train midwives and primary health workers • Support obstetrics and neonatal care

THINGS TO DO AND THINK ABOUT

Look at the table above. What specific rights are these agencies protecting and promoting in other countries?

DON'T FORGET

Always try and link the work carried out by the UN to the needs of the country.

FACT

Libya had a representative at the special session meeting.

VIDEO LINK

For more on the Arab Spring, watch the clip at www.brightredbooks.net/N5ModernStudies.

ONLINE

Read the article 'A Climate of Change' for more at www.brightredbooks.net/N5ModernStudies.

FACT

Regardless of the dangerous situation the WFP provided 2.6 million meals to Libyan refugees and reached 1.5 million people. This was the first time they had cooked meals in camps.

ONLINE TEST

Check how much you have learned about human rights in Libya and the UN online at www.brightredbooks.net/N5ModernStudies.

HUMAN RIGHTS AND INTERNATIONAL PRESSURE GROUPS

As we have learned from the previous section, human rights are promoted and protected by international alliances such as the UN. However, other organisations also support the development of human rights across the world. These organisations take the form of pressure groups and have members from different countries coming together to take action to prevent human rights abuses. They can form to address local, national or international issues. In this section we are going to look at the role the international pressure group Amnesty International has had in protecting human rights since its founding in 1961.

ONLINE

For more about what Amnesty International does check out its website at www.brightredbooks.net/ N5ModernStudies.

VIDEO LINK

Check out the Amnesty International videos page at www.brightredbooks.net/ N5ModernStudies to learn more.

AMNESTY INTERNATIONAL

'We are a campaigning organisation; it's what we do. Our purpose is to protect people wherever justice, fairness, freedom and truth are denied.' Amnesty International website.

The notion that ordinary people can influence the world and as a result make a tremendous difference is the founding principle of Amnesty International. When the group was originally formed the focus was on helping people who had been unfairly imprisoned. Over the years it has contributed to the release of thousands of prisoners all over the world. Since its creation the group has expanded its area of work and campaigned against a wider range of human rights abuses, for example cases of torture, unexplained disappearances, political killings, the death penalty and gay rights abuses. Amnesty International is an independent organisation that is not controlled, influenced or financed by any government. By 2005 it had become the largest independent human rights group in the world, with 1.8 million members. It has continued to grow and membership in 2013 was over 3 million.

In order to defend human rights Amnesty International has two main strategies:
1　Develop awareness through education projects based on the principles of the UN Declaration of Human Rights.
2　Conduct research and challenge specific cases of human rights abuses across the world.

CAMPAIGNS

Amnesty International has several campaigns running at the same time. However, one of its long-standing focuses has been to abolish the death penalty in every country in the world. It believes that using this form of punishment breaks the right to life and the right not be tortured or subjected to cruel, inhuman or degrading punishment.

Despite Amnesty International's campaign the use of the death penalty does not break international law nor is it seen to breach human rights when carried out correctly. Amnesty International has discovered that the number of countries that have the death penalty and the number that actually use it is declining. In 2011, 198 countries still had the death penalty as a punishment, but only 21 actually used it. Out of these 21 countries three-quarters of all death sentences are carried out in three countries: Iran, Iraq and Saudi Arabia. Discrimination and incorrect sentencing are common in death penalty cases and it is therefore not always used correctly.

Stance on death penalty	Number of countries	Example countries
Without death penalty	97	Denmark, Cambodia, Spain, Poland
For extreme crimes	8	Brazil, Chile, Peru, Israel
Not executed in past 10 years	35	Tunisia, Malawi, Madagascar, Sri Lanka
Death penalty	58	USA, Sudan, China, Cuba

contd

THE DEATH PENALTY AND CHILDREN

It is illegal to execute children and doing so breaks international law. Amnesty International campaigns to help to combat this abuse of human rights. Amnesty International has recorded 62 cases of child execution in eight different countries since 2000. In 2009 children were executed in Saudi Arabia, Iran and Sudan, and children were held on death row in Sudan, Nigeria, Uganda, Burma and Yemen.

Case studies

Name	Behnoud Shojaee	Abdulrahman Zakaria Mohammed
Country	Iran	Sudan
Year of conviction	2006	2007
Age at conviction	17	17
Year of execution	2009	2009
Crime	Intervened in a fight and stabbed another boy who as a result bled to death. Shojaee confessed and handed himself into the police	Murder and robbery

Crimes such as murder, terrorism, rape, drug trafficking, adultery and treason are punishable by death in both Iran and Sudan. Although the Sudan Child Act of 2010 states that no child under 18 can be executed, there is often controversy when determining the individual's real age. Despite international law it has been reported that Iran has more than 100 individuals under 18 on death row. Government officials state that they still abide by international law as they do not carry out executions until prisoners have turned 18.

AMNESTY INTERNATIONAL'S WORK

There are different actions that Amnesty International will take to prevent the use of the death penalty for both children and adults.

- Petition for the release of individual prisoners.

- Carry out research to create reports. These reports allow trends and individual cases to be identified and shared with the international community.

- Work with other human rights pressure groups such as the World Coalition Against the Death Penalty. This organisation brings together over 70 pressure groups, with Amnesty International being the founding member.

- Work with the UN to prohibit use of the death penalty.

THINGS TO DO AND THINK ABOUT

1 Would you consider joining a human rights pressure group? Give at least three reasons to explain your answer.

2 What forms of punishment do young offenders receive in Scotland?

3 Debate: Do you think the death penalty should be used as a form of punishment? Do you think it should be used on children and adults?

4 Using the Amnesty International website, try to find out about the different campaigns that it is currently running.

HUMAN RIGHTS AND LOCAL RESPONSES

RECAP

So far this chapter has highlighted some of the human rights problems that exist across the world and the groups that try and address those problems. We have covered the work of the UN and the international charity organisation Amnesty International. This final section will explain the ways in which local people have taken action to improve their own human rights. We will be looking at two case studies:

1   women's rights in Afghanistan   2   Pussy Riot's fight in Russia

VIDEO LINK

Check out the clip about education in Afghanistan at www.brightredbooks.net/N5ModernStudies.

AFGHANISTAN: THE SITUATION

The Taliban are an extreme Islamist organisation that gained control of a large part of Afghanistan in 1994. When they were in power they enforced strict Islamic law, and women and girls were denied a wide range of rights. During their rule they were denied an education, employment and health care, and had to be accompanied by a man wherever they went. After the invasion of Afghanistan, led by the USA, in 2001 the Tailban were removed from power and the rights of women have gradually improved. They are now permitted to work again, with many becoming politicians, lawyers and doctors. The new constitution implemented in 2004 states 'the citizens of Afghanistan – whether man or woman – have equal rights and duties before the law'. Despite this, many women in rural areas are heavily controlled by their families and denied human rights. Although there have been changes in the law, changes in attitudes have been more difficult to achieve, for example women are forced into unwanted marriages and schools with female students have been burned down.

LOCAL ACTION

May 2013 protests

When a 22-year-old woman was publicly executed in Kabul after being accused of committing adultery many Afghan citizens took to the streets. The protestors shouted 'We want justice' and gathered outside the UN building. Protests like this one often have a big impact because they raise awareness of the situation, which forces authorities to take action. The execution was viewed as a crime and the authorities planned to find the people responsible.

Afghanaid

This is a charity organisation that focuses solely on Afghanistan. One of its aims is to improve the position of women in their local areas. Many women have successfully taken advantage of the support offered by this local charity and as a result have acted as positive role models for other Afghan women. For example, an 18-year-old woman named Shahnaz Jan took part in a business project offered by Afghanaid. She now runs her own cosmetics shop, allowing her to earn her own income. Her story is an inspiration for young women, who hopefully will follow in her footsteps.

Revolutionary Association of the Women of Afghanistan

The Revolutionary Association of the Women of Afghanistan (RAWA) was set up in 1977 to improve peace, freedom, democracy and rights for women within Afghanistan. Its priority is to help women who have been affected by war and denied their human rights by other groups. They have educational, financial and health care projects, for example they have mobile health teams in eight provinces. These groups provide free care for those who cannot afford it and hold free first-aid courses for local women.

PUSSY RIOT: THE SITUATION

Pussy Riot are an all-girl punk band from Russia who are known for their bright balaclavas and controversial lyrics. The band sing songs that voice opinions against Russia's president, Vladimir Putin, and the system of government in Russia. After they carried out a flashmob in an Orthodox cathedral in Moscow on 21 February 2012, the band were arrested and eventually received a 2-year jail sentence. The band were charged with hooliganism and racial hatred, and it was believed that they were a threat to the public. One member, Yekaterina Samutsevich, was released after an appeal, but the remaining band members are still in prison.

However, this is no simple case; the band members generated great controversy throughout Russia and many other countries around the world. Pro Pussy Riot supporters believe that the girls are being punished for speaking out against the president rather than generating religious hatred. They believe that the punishment they received was too harsh and highlighted the lack of the political freedom of speech in Russia. The international community shares similar views, with America, the UK and the EU stating that the punishment was 'disproportionate'.

ACTION

Methods:
- protests
- fundraisers
- petitions
- letter writing
- celebrity support.

Soon after the girls were placed in custody protests erupted in Russia, with over 15,000 people campaigning for their release. Many people recognised that the act was disrespectful but believed the punishment went against their human rights. Letters were sent by the head of the church requesting the case be dropped and groups opposing Putin claim the stunt was 'idiotic but not dangerous'.

The campaign grew even stronger when it was revealed that the members were facing a possible 7-year jail sentence for their crimes. This attracted international attention, with protests being held in Paris, Kiev, Belgrade, Berlin, London, Dublin and Barcelona. Within Russia over 25,000 citizens requesting their release and artists' freedom of speech signed a petition. The public also showed their support during the trial as hundreds of people gathered outside the courtroom.

Although Amnesty International also campaign for Pussy Riot the response and the reaction from Russian citizens propelled the case into the media and is a good example of people fighting for the rights of others.

THINGS TO DO AND THINK ABOUT

1   Imagine you are a journalist who has been sent to report on what life is like for women under Taliban rule. Write a story explaining what you discover.

2   Describe, in detail, the different methods that Pussy Riot campaigners used to fight for their freedom.

3   Can you think of any other ways that local people could support campaigns like these?

VIDEO LINK

Check out the clip about the Pussy Riot situation for more at www.brightredbooks.net/N5ModernStudies.

FACT

There are actually about 13 members of Pussy Riot, who frequently change.

FACT

Madonna and Franz Ferdinand campaigned for Pussy Riot during their concerts in Moscow.

ONLINE TEST

Check how much you have learned about human rights and local response online at www.brightredbooks.net/N5ModernStudies.

DON'T FORGET

There are also groups that have been set up to fight against these campaigns.

CHILD SOLDIERS

WHAT IS A CHILD SOLDIER?

The international community has decided that a child soldier is any person under the age of 18 that is involved in an armed force or group. It doesn't matter if they are part of a rebel or government-supported organisation. Child soldiers can fulfil a range of roles, not just that of a fighter, for example cook, spy, porter, messenger or sex slave. In 2000 Child Soldiers International revealed that child soldiers existed in the majority of wars across the world. Other studies insist that the numbers are actually higher than this at around 250,000 and as young as 8. The number of child soldiers is difficult to record as the number frequently changes and countries are reluctant to tell the truth.

VIDEO LINK

Check out the campaign video from Invisible Children, a charity campaigning to help victims of war in Uganda at www.brightredbooks.net/N5ModernStudies.

WHY SHOULD WE LEARN ABOUT CHILD SOLDIERS?

Despite national and international laws that control the age at which individuals can fight and the age at which they can lawfully be recruited, many countries still permit the use of child soldiers. Countries either recruit and use child soldiers in their forces and organisations or can do nothing to stop rebel groups using them.

These types of actions go against treaties, laws and promises that countries have made and they deny children their fundamental rights. Life as a child soldier is extremely difficult and can result in long-term physical and psychological problems.

Afghanistan	The Taliban use child soldiers in conflicts and reports have revealed that they are used in suicide attacks
Myanmar	Children aged 11 have been forced to join the national army
Colombia	Rebel groups have been found to use thousands of children during conflicts
India	Children aged 6 have been kidnapped and forced to join armed groups
Sudan	Both the army and rebel groups have been found guilty of using child soldiers

ONLINE

Check out the Human Rights Watch website at www.brightredbooks.net/N5ModernStudies.

LAWS

A range of national and international agreements have been made in order to prevent and protect child soldiers across the world.

Convention on the Rights of the Child (1989)

After being agreed on by the UN General Assembly in 1989 this Convention came into place in 1990. Currently all UN member states have signed and ratified the Convention apart from Somalia and the USA.

The Convention includes 45 Articles outlining the rights of the child. Article 1 clarifies that a child is any person under the age 18. The Convention prevents anyone under the age of 15 being recruited or used in armed conflicts.

Optional Protocol to the Convention on the Rights of the Child on the Involvement of Children in Armed Conflict (2000)

In 2000 there were two Optional Protocols added to the Convention. The first required the minimum age of individuals directly involved in armed conflicts and compulsory recruitment to be raised to 18. The second protocol prohibited the sexual exploitation and abuse of children. These changes were the result of the international community's continued commitment to protecting children.

International criminal law (1998)

The International Criminal Court deals with war crimes, crimes against

FACT

The Convention on the Rights of the Child came into being in the UK in 1992, after it was signed in 1990.

contd

humanity and genocide. Under the Rome Statute (1998), the recruitment and use of children under the age of 15 is a war crime. This applies to both government and non-government groups.

International labour law

In 1973 the International Labour Organisation required countries to abolish child labour and set the age limit for work that may impact on health and safety at 18. In 1999 this was developed further with the Worst Forms of Child Labour Convention. This Convention outlined participation in armed conflicts as the worst form of child labour and therefore it should not be a role for anyone under the age of 18.

International humanitarian law (1977)

Four international treaties were created in 1949 to control and decrease the effects of armed conflicts. These treaties are referred to as the Geneva Convention and their priority is to protect those who are not partaking in the conflict. A protocol added in 1977 declared 15 to be the age at which individuals can be recruited and used in conflicts.

African Charter on the Rights and Welfare of the Child (1999)

This is the only regional charter in the world to include sections regarding child soldiers. The charter states that no-one under the age of 18 is permitted to be directly involved in armed conflicts.

PROBLEMS WITH THE LAWS

Louder Than Words (2012), a report carried out by Child Soldiers International, discovered that despite these wide-ranging international laws and treaties countries are still failing to protect children from becoming child soldiers.

The table below outlines the main problems with the laws regarding child soldiers.

Point	Explain	Example
Some countries still permit the use of children for war in certain circumstances.	Although the country has agreed to the specification in treaties and international law it has adapted them slightly.	Vietnam law states that no child shall be used in armed conflict unless there is a significant threat to national independence.
Children in military schools can be involved in conflict situations.	In these cases the government require more personnel and have defended their actions by claiming that the personnel did not require arms.	In 2009, 5609 cadets and military school children were involved in an operation to bring down drug gangs in Mexico. As the operation did not involve weapons the government insisted that they had not broken international law.
Recruiters are unaware of laws and have recruitment targets.	Although heads of government forces understand the international requirements this is not always passed onto the people who are carrying out the recruitment process. If recruiters are being rewarded for meeting targets, they are more likely to target children.	The Democratic Republic of Congo uses cash incentives to encourage recruiters to increase numbers.
Mistakes about the exact age of individuals can result in children being recruited and used in armed conflict.	A person's age is usually determined by using their birth certificate, but a study carried out by UNICEF discovered that 51 million births are not registered each year and that numbers of unregistered births are higher in areas where conflict is common. Armies will use alternative methods to decide on age, which are often unreliable.	School registration, height and weight have been used to determine age in Uganda, but errors are common.

THINGS TO DO AND THINK ABOUT

1   Give three reasons why we should learn about child soldiers.

2   Create a timeline showing the international agreements with regards to child soldiers.

LIFE AS A CHILD SOLDIER

In this section we are going to investigate why children become soldiers and look at some real-life experiences of child soldiers. Children end up involved in armed conflicts for a range of reasons. To help understand the world issues of child soldiers this section will answer the following key questions:

- Why become a child soldier?
- Why do groups want child soldiers?
- What is it like being a child soldier?

WHY BECOME A CHILD SOLDIER?

Forced

ONLINE

Find out more by following the link to the Child Soldiers International webpage at www.brightredbooks.net/ N5ModernStudies.

Rebel groups or recruitment teams from government forces may take children by forcing them or using violence. They might be abducted during the night and dragged away from their families or even taken when they are in school. Families are often threatened with violence or even death if they do not let the children join the group. Zaw Tun from Somalia was forced to join the army as his family could not pay what the recruiters demanded:

'I was recruited by force, against my will [...] army recruitment unit arrived next morning at my village and demanded two new recruits. Those who could not pay 3000 kyats had to join the army ...'

Volunteer

This might be hard to imagine but some children want to join armed groups. Their standard of living may be very low and the promise of food, clothing and shelter can be very appealing when they are struggling to survive from day to day. They might also already be caught up in the conflict and think they would be safer to join a group who may protect them. Their family and friends might already be in the group and therefore they join to stay with them. Some girls join groups to get away from domestic violence at home.

WHY DO GROUPS WANT CHILDREN?

Armed groups recruit children into their ranks because children are very easy to control. They often are too young to understand the conflict and what they are doing, therefore they are easy to manipulate. If children are recruited at a very young age and stay with the group a long time a sense of loyalty is likely to develop. They are much less likely to rebel against leaders and are more likely to follow instructions. Children eat less food and will be happy with a smaller amount of pay therefore they cost the group less money. Children also have a lower sense of danger and are therefore more willing to fight than older soldiers. The risk of children running away is slim because they have nowhere else to go.

WHAT IS IT LIKE BEING A CHILD SOLDIER?

Life as a child soldier is very traumatic. Even though children may have been promised food and shelter, this is often not the case and they continue to live in poverty.

Both boys and girls will receive military training. The development in technology has meant that weapons have became lighter and easier for young children to carry and use, for example the AK47.

contd

Children are taught not only to kill their enemy but also how to capture and torture them. This has long-term psychological effects on children and many struggle to recover from their violent experiences.

Experiences of child soldiers

An account provided by the charity organisation Ajedi-Ka (Projet Enfants Soldats):

'Life forced me to become a child soldier'

A young boy has shared his experiences of being a child soldier with a local charity. He explained that after he was abducted he was trained to kidnap, torture and kill his enemy. This involved learning how to cut off people's ears and feet, and then remove their eyes and finally their hearts. Within the group girls also received army training but were mainly used as cooks or sexually abused. All the children were scared and were not given enough food or medicine when they were sick or injured.

CASE STUDY: DEMOCRATIC REPUBLIC OF CONGO

Since its independence in 1960 the Democratic Republic of Congo (DRC) has been plagued with war and conflict.

The DRC has many natural resources that make it wealthy, such as diamonds, gold, copper, cobalt and zinc. However, the weak infrastructure and corruption of the country has meant that the country has been unable to turn these resources into prosperity. The country has been split into different groups who fight for control over these resources.

In 1994 the Hutu people of Rwanda massacred the Tutsi people and this had a significant effect on the DRC. When the Hutu people lost power in Rwanda they escaped to the DRC and joined forces with the DRC leader Mobutu. Together the National Army and the Hutu groups began to fight against the Tutsi people who lived in the DRC. The Tutsi people were able to seize power from Mobutu and a man named Laurent Kabila became the President. This wasn't the end, however, and the Hutu people, backed by Rwanda's government, continued to fight against Kabila. This war lasted from 1998 to 2003.

It has been estimated that more than 5.5 million people died in the conflict from fighting, starvation or disease.

Even though the fighting ended officially in 2003 the east of the country continued to experience conflict, and rebels continued to fight against government forces and UN peacekeepers. In 2012 relations between the DRC and Rwanda crumbled, and more rebel groups emerged in the east.

Despite the DRC signing and ratifying the Optional Protocol in November 2001 both government-backed forces and rebel groups have recruited and used children in these conflicts. Progress was made when the war ended in 2003 and thousands of children were discharged from the armed forces. However, when conflicts broke out again groups turned to children to fill their ranks. An estimated 7000 child soldiers were still members of government forces in 2008.

Even though the use of child soldiers is illegal the government is not completely enforcing its policies. It has failed to fully explore suspected cases and therefore groups go unpunished.

THINGS TO DO AND THINK ABOUT

1 Write a creative piece about the story of a child soldier. Consider the reasons they became a child soldier, the group they joined and the jobs they had to do.

VIDEO LINK

Watch the short film for more on the child soldiers in the DRC at www.brightredbooks.net/N5ModernStudies.

FACT

The DRC's name was changed from Congo to Zaire after Joseph Mobutu took over in 1965. It was President Laurent Kabila that named the country the Democratic Republic of Congo.

DON'T FORGET

Child soldiers have many roles other than fighting.

ONLINE TEST

Check how much you have learned about child soldiers online at www.brightredbooks.net/N5ModernStudies.

CHILD SOLDIERS: DEALING WITH THE ISSUE

This section explains the ways groups are trying to solve the problem of children being used in armed conflicts. Many different local and international organisations work hard to stop children becoming soldiers, provide support when they leave armed groups and raise international awareness of the problems.

LOCAL RESPONSES

The charity group Ajedi-Ka has been set up within the DRC to concentrate on three areas:

1 poverty   2 environment   3 child soldiers.

In order to tackle the issue of child soldiers the group promotes an awareness of the issue in local communities and provides long-term support to children who have returned from armed groups. Its work therefore deals with the issue of successfully reintegrating children back into their community.

Project: Demobilisation, Reintegration and Rehabilitation of Child Soldiers

This project involves setting up a system of support for children who return home. Within each village that is part of the project a committee for child protection is set up. The aim of the committee is to help children address psychological issues and create positive relationships with those in their community. The charity also funds education projects for child soldiers and helps with the development of small-scale business management so they can become self-sufficient. The project works with the Open Society Institute teaching girls self-confidence and leadership skills. This means they are more likely to be able to break out of the cycle of abuse.

INTERNATIONAL RESPONSES

Child Soldiers International is an international charity working to prevent children from being recruited and used in armed conflict.

It aims to:
- end the military recruitment of children (people below the age of 18) or their use in armed conflict by government armies or non-state armed groups.
- release unlawfully recruited children.
- promote child soldiers' successful reintegration when they return home.
- ensure that child recruiters are brought to justice.

The organisation's work is based on the "child soldiers treaty" – a human rights treaty prohibiting the use of child soldiers, which more than two thirds of the world's governments have pledged to uphold.

Projects

Child Soldiers International has country programmes in Chad, the Democratic Republic of the Congo (DRC), Myanmar and Thailand, where it works in partnership with local activists and organisations to research, analyse and lobby for change – locally, nationally and internationally. It is running a campaign to raise the recruitment age in the UK, one of the few countries which still permits 16 year olds to enter the armed forces. Based on its country work and analysis, Child Soldiers International proposes practical, workable solutions – rooted firmly in human rights law – to support and strengthen the global movement to end the use of children in war.

ONLINE

Have a look at the Ajedi-Ka website at www.brightredbooks.net/N5ModernStudies.

ONLINE

Read about the International Day Against the Use of Child Soldiers in the Democratic Republic of Congo at www.brightredbooks.net/N5ModernStudies.

THE UN: CHILDREN AND ARMED CONFLICT

Special Representative of the Secretary-General for Children and Armed Conflict: 'To promote and protect the rights of all children affected by armed conflict.'

This UN organisation was set up in 1996 after the World Summit for Children and aims to raise awareness and work with other groups to help children.

So, what does it do?

Sharing information

The UN carries out extensive research and monitoring into crimes involving children in armed conflicts. Its yearly reports focus on the following areas:

- killing of children
- illegal recruitment of children
- sexual abuse involving children
- attacks on schools or hospitals
- kidnapping of children
- humanitarian aid for children.

The findings published in the report will support decisions made by the UN Security Council.

Identifying offenders

The process of identifying offenders has been in place since 2002 and lists groups who are using or illegally recruiting children in armed conflicts. This draws international attention to the groups and forces them to make changes. The most recent report revealed that 57 groups in 15 different conflicts have been using children illegally. Out of the 57, 17 have been on the list for five continuous years. The only way to get removed from the list is to create an action plan to address the problem. This system has been relatively successful, with 5 governments and 12 independent groups recently signing a promise to change.

PROGRESS OF CHILDREN AND ARMED CONFLICT

Compulsory recruitment

Groups have been campaigning to increase the compulsory recruitment age to 18 and many countries have changed their systems to enforce this policy, for example Paraguay, Croatia, Norway and Serbia have all changed their age limits. In addition there are now fewer than 20 countries that recruit individuals aged 16, including India, Iran, Brazil, Canada and the UK.

Success stories

Myanmar, February 2013

Myanmar's government upheld the promise it made to the UN to free child soldiers and help them return home. In February 24 children were released and went back home.

Thomas Lubanga Dyilo, March 2012

Thomas Lubanga Dyilo was heavily involved in the conflict within the DRC and recruited child soldiers as young as 7 to fight for his cause in 2003. In March 2012 the International Criminal Court found him guilty of recruiting child soldiers, torture, rape and ethnic genocide, and was sentenced to 14 years of imprisonment.

THINGS TO DO AND THINK ABOUT

1   You have been tasked with the job of creating a website to highlight the issue of child soldiers. You should include the following points:
- the number of child soldiers and where in the world they are
- the laws that exist to protect child soldiers
- why children join armed forces and what groups use them
- what life is like for child soldiers
- what different groups are doing to try and help.

You should consider the layout of your website, pictures, contact information and any extra features you can think of.

VIDEO LINK

Watch the clip about children and armed conflict for more at www.brightredbooks.net/N5ModernStudies.

ONLINE

Visit the Children and Armed Conflict link for more at www.brightredbooks.net/N5ModernStudies.

DON'T FORGET

You can help raise awareness of child soldiers in your school and contribute to the Child Soldiers International campaign.

ONLINE TEST

Take the 'Dealing with the issue' test at www.brightredbooks.net/N5ModernStudies.

INEQUALITY 1

MILLENNIUM DEVELOPMENT GOALS

After a three-day UN World Summit in 2000 the international community agreed on eight specific development targets. These targets are referred to as the Millennium Development Goals (MDGs) and are detailed in the UN Millennium Declaration. Ever since the goals were decided, countries throughout the world have been taking steps to ensure that they are met by the target year of 2015.

1 Eradicate extreme poverty and hunger.
2 Achieve universal primary education.
3 Promote gender equality and empower women.
4 Reduce child mortality.
5 Improve maternal health.
6 Combat HIV/AIDS, malaria and other diseases.
7 Ensure environmental sustainability.
8 Set up global partnership of development.

Secretary-General Kofi Annan: 'It lies in your power, and therefore is your responsibility, to reach the goals you have defined.'

We are now going to investigate the issue of extreme hunger and the progress that has been made towards meeting this MDG. The first half of this goal is to halve the percentage of hungry people in the world by 2015.

RIGHT TO FOOD

The Universal Declaration of Human Rights Article 25 outlines that everyone has the right to a reasonable standard of living, including enough food.

The problems

There are many different problems associated with food shortages. Although famines have a devastating effect on countries, they only account for 10% of the food shortage related deaths. Many people in the world face everyday challenges accessing enough of the correct food.

Problem	Definition
Hunger	Consuming fewer than 1800 calories a day
Undernutrition	Shortage of the correct nutrients such as vitamins or proteins Accounts for 35% of all under-5 mortalities
Malnutrition	Can be either undernutrition or overnutrition Overnutrition occurs without a correctly balanced diet
Food security	Not having a consistent supply of food
Famine	Declared if: • 20% of the population have access to less than 2100 calories • 30% of children are malnourished • 2/10,000 adult and 4/10,000 child deaths per day

Source: UN Food and Agriculture Organisation, World Food Programme, International Food Policy Research Centre.

The Food and Agriculture Organisation (FAO) discovered that in 2012, 870 million people across the world were 'chronically undernourished'. Most of these people lived in less developed countries. Lack of sufficient food has a knock-on effect in a person's life: he/she is more likely to get ill, have poor concentration and suffer from fatigue. This means he/she will find it more difficult to, for example, study at school or to get a job.

FACT

The Millennium Summit was the largest meeting of international leaders ever.

ONLINE

Learn more about the Millennium Development Goals at www.brightredbooks.net/N5ModernStudies.

FACT

A third of all food production, 1.3 billion tonnes, worldwide is wasted each year.

WHO SUFFERS?

Calculating hunger levels is a complex task involving many different factors. To judge the levels of hunger in the world the International Food Policy Institute created the Global Hunger Index. Countries are rated between 0 and 100, with 0 being no hunger. If a country scores between 20 and 29.9 the situation is 'alarming'; scoring over 30 is classed as 'extremely alarming'.

The index considers the following factors:
- the number of undernourished people in the population
- the number of children under 5 who are underweight
- the mortality rate for children under 5.

Global Hunger Index 2012 Results

There are significant regional differences:
- South-East Asia and sub-Saharan Africa have the highest ratings.
- 17 countries have a rating 20 or higher, for example Sudan, India and Bangladesh.
- Three countries have a rating 30 or higher: Burundi, Eritrea and Haiti.
- The lower a country's gross national income (GNI) the higher its Global Hunger Index, for example Mozambique had a Global Hunger Index of 26 with a GNI of 1000 international dollars and China had a Global Hunger Index of 5 and a GNI of 62,500 international dollars.

There can be problems when obtaining the data needed to calculate a rating therefore not all countries have a rating. For example, the DRC has previously received the highest rating, but there was insignificant data to produce a result in 2012.

REASONS FOR HUNGER

Poor farming

Out of the 852 million hungry people in the world almost 50% of them are farmers who are unable to harvest enough food to either eat or sell.

Conflicts

Countries that are involved in conflicts or experiencing civil wars are much more likely to have high hunger ratings. This is because destroying land and cutting off food supplies are tactics often used by groups.

Gender inequality

Women are more likely to suffer from hunger than men; 60% of chronically hungry people are women. This is a result of poor technology, poor training and being deprived ownership of land, for example in 2009 in sub-Saharan Africa only 40% of women had access to land compared to 85% in Central and Eastern Europe and Central Asia.

FACT

In 2012, 16 million people were undernourished in developed countries.

THINGS TO DO AND THINK ABOUT

Using the information on these pages, and pages 118–119, create your own hunger campaign. Consider the following points:
- What is your campaign slogan?
- Why should people support your campaign?
- How will you share information about your campaign?
- How could people get involved in your campaign?
- What campaign materials will you produce?

ONLINE TEST

Revise your knowledge of the world issue of hunger at www.brightredbooks.net/N5ModernStudies.

INEQUALITY 2

ACTION

VIDEO LINK

Watch the video message from Zero Hunger Challenge at www.brightredbooks.net/N5ModernStudies.

There are many organisations that have the aim of stopping world hunger. Other alliances have also formed, for example the World Food Summit and Zero Hunger Challenge.

World Food Summit

In 1996 180 countries agreed to eliminate hunger and halve the number of undernourished people in the world by 2015. Progress towards achieving these goals was assessed in 2002 and the International Alliance Against Hunger was formed.

Zero Hunger Challenge

This is an alliance of a range of agencies such as the project Think-Eat-Save, FAO and the International Fund for Agriculture. The challenge is to ensure 100% access to enough food, no stunted children under the age of two, maintainable food structures, no food waste and 100% increase in food output.

CASE STUDY: THE HUNGER PROJECT: ERADICATING WORLD HUNGER

The Hunger Project has 380,000 volunteer leaders who work in over 8700 villages in 11 countries in South-East Asia, sub-Saharan Africa and Latin America. Within eight African countries they have set up over 115 epicentre communities. These epicentres are groups of villages that run activities to meet the needs of local people. Each epicentre is given support to get started but then the local people take over and run the activities themselves.

PROGRESS

DON'T FORGET

There are many different organisations and charities that are working to overcome global food inequalities.

In June 2013 the FAO announced that 38 countries had met the target ahead of schedule. Overall hunger rates have decreased. However, there are still 870 million people throughout the world who are undernourished. Out of those 38 countries 18 also met the World Food Summit's goal to reduce the number of undernourished people.

Countries that have achieved the target

- Algeria
- Angola
- Bangladesh
- Benin
- Brazil
- Cambodia
- Cameroon
- Chile
- Dominican Republic
- Fiji
- Honduras
- Indonesia
- Jordan
- Malawi
- Maldives
- Niger
- Nigeria
- Panama
- Togo
- Uruguay

Countries that have also achieved the World Food Summit Goal

- Armenia
- Azerbaijan
- Cuba
- Djibouti
- Georgia
- Ghana
- Guyana
- Kuwait
- Kyrgyzstan
- Nicaragua
- Peru
- Saint Vincent and the Grenadines
- Samoa
- Sao Tome and Principe
- Thailand
- Turkmenistan
- Venezuela
- Vietnam

contd

As there are still 852 million hungry people living in less developed countries world hunger is still an issue, despite this progress. Not everywhere is experiencing a decline, for example North Korea, Burundi, Swaziland, Comoros, Cote D'Ivoire and Botswana all experienced an increase in their Global Hunger Index rating since the Millennium Development Goals were created.

THE IMPORTANCE OF EDUCATION

Education is something that thousands of children across the world take for granted. They perhaps don't understand its value, as it is part of normal everyday life. However, when you study the impact of education and the levels of access to it across world its importance is very clear.

The significance of education and the inequalities that exist have been recognised by the international community and made a priority in development plans.

Improves health

Children who attend school will also have access to health care. Many schools will administer important vaccinations and provide additional care if a child is unwell. Children will also increase their awareness of health issues, which may prevent them from getting illnesses such as HIV/AIDS.

Decreases poverty

The World Bank has discovered that education is one of the biggest contributing factors to overcoming poverty. They have focused on using education as a pathway out of poverty since 1962. If children receive an education they gain valuable life skills that improve their employment opportunities and allow them to contribute to the economy.

Impact for girls

UNICEF has discovered that girls who have received an education are more likely to produce and raise healthier children. This is because there is a higher chance they will marry at an older age and also decide to have smaller families. Having a smaller family means that the children will be healthier and more likely to receive an education themselves. Educated girls will also have a better knowledge of how to care for their own children and deal with any health problems. Mothers who have been in education have a higher tendency to pursue health information throughout their pregnancy and make sure children are correctly vaccinated.

 THINGS TO DO AND THINK ABOUT

What are the different problems caused by the lack of correct food?

 ONLINE TEST

Revise your knowledge of the world issue of education at www.brightredbooks.net/N5ModernStudies.

INEQUALITY 3

ONLINE

Find out more about UNESCO's work in world education at www.brightredbooks.net/N5ModernStudies.

VIDEO LINK

Check out UNESCO's YouTube channel for more at www.brightredbooks.net/N5ModernStudies.

INEQUALITIES IN EDUCATION

Access to education

A study carried out by UNESCO discovered that there were 102 million children not in school throughout the world. Out of this total 43% live in sub-Saharan Africa. It has also been discovered that the majority of children that are not in school live in areas affected by conflict or natural disaster.

Equal access

Equal access to education is also a key issue: two out of three countries experience gender inequalities within their education systems, with boys being more likely to attend school than girls, for example in 1990 for every 100 literate males there were 90 females. Although that had improved to 100:95 in 2010, a gender gap still exists. In 2011 two-thirds of the 793 million adults who did not have a basic level of literacy were female.

Quality of education

Even when children are attending school in less-developed countries there are huge differences in the experiences they have. Schools are often understaffed and overcrowded, for example in the Central African Republic some schools have as many as 84 pupils per class. There is also a shortage of resources: in Cameroon up to 12 pupils may have to share a textbook. Schools are often of a low quality, for example in Chad 75% of schools have no water, sanitation or electricity. If universal primary education is to be achieved UNESCO predicts that an extra 2 million teachers will have to put in place by 2015.

DON'T FORGET

UNESCO stands for United Nations Educational, Scientific and Cultural Organisation.

VIDEO LINK

Watch the clip at www.brightredbooks.net/N5ModernStudies for more on Education for All.

FACT

Now that more and more children are completing primary school there is an increasing demand for secondary schools.

FIGHTING FOR EDUCATION

UNESCO

The UN specialised agency UNESCO is committed to supporting the development of education across the world. The organisation works with governments and other international groups to try and achieve the second Millennium Development Goal of universal primary education and the targets outlined in the Education for All agreement.

Education for All is an international agreement headed by UNESCO to ensure that all children, adolescents and adults have access to basic education. To achieve this it has been agreed there should be free compulsory primary education, gender equality, an improvement in the quality of education and an increase in literacy rates among adults. In total 164 governments have agreed to meet this target by 2015 (the same deadline as the Millennium Development Goals).

Case study: Haiti Earthquake 2010, dealing with natural disaster

To support Haiti after the earthquake hit and demolished 90% of the schools in the area UNESCO helped to produce and distribute emergency lesson packs. To support the children affected they helped train over 3000 school teachers to deal with trauma and stress. They also managed to collect 6000 donated books and distributed them around camps.

UNICEF

UNICEF is the biggest organisation that campaigns and supports projects to meet the needs of children across the world. Its aim is to ensure that every child receives

contd

the rights outlined in the UN Convention on the Rights of the Child. They have been involved in a range of projects that focus on improving education.

Case study: Work in Uganda

Within the mountains of Karamoja in Uganda there is a collection of villages that are home to the Ik population. Because the area is so isolated, they have limited schools and resources close by. To deal with this problem UNICEF supported the building of a new primary school and projects within the school such as a feeding programme.

PROGRESS

There are now more children than ever before receiving an education:
* Between 1999 and 2008 an extra 52 million children were enrolled in primary school.
* Less-developed countries have seen an increase in enrolments from 82% in 1999 to 90% in 2010.

Afghanistan

By 2008 Afghanistan had 2.2 million girls in school. This is a huge increase from 2001, when this figure was just 15,000.

Vietnam

Vietnam's government has increased its spending on education significantly, from 7% in 1986 to 20% in 2001. This shows that the government is recognising the significance of education and is willing to work to improve the situation.

Ethiopia

Ethiopia has boosted its percentage of primary registration by around 15% since 2003.

Yemen

In 2009 57% of girls finished primary school in Yemen compared to just 28% in 2001 (source: The World Bank).

There is still a lot of work to be done globally with regards to education. UNESCO discovered that in 2011 out of the 67 million children who were still not in primary school 53% were girls and 43% lived in sub-Saharan Africa. The number of children starting school has significantly increased, but high dropout rates mean that not everyone will finish. Less-developed countries still struggle to provide enough teachers and resources to support the same level of education as in developed countries. Problems still exist in areas affected by conflict and natural disasters.

 DON'T FORGET

Education is a universal human right and is outlined in the Universal Declaration of Human Rights, Article 26.

 ONLINE TEST

Revise your knowledge of the world issue of education at www.brightredbooks.net/N5ModernStudies.

 THINGS TO DO AND THINK ABOUT

Consider the following points:

a What do you gain from being in school? Make a list/mind map.

b What would you do if you didn't go to school?

c What would your life be like in 10 years if you had never been to school?

INEQUALITY: CHILD MORTALITY

This section addresses the international health inequality of child mortality. Child mortality rates can reveal a range of social and economic problems, including a poor healthcare system. The issue of child mortality has been recognised by the international community and decreasing the number of children dying under the age of 5 by two-thirds is the fourth Millennium Development Goal.

To learn about child mortality we will focus on the following questions:

- What is it?
- What areas are affected?
- What progress has been made in overcoming the issue?

WHAT IS IT?

Child mortality is when a child dies before he/she reaches his/her 5th birthday. In 2011 6.9 million children had died before reaching the age of 5. UNICEF discovered that 21 children under 5 die every minute from a reason that could be dealt with, for example 70% of child deaths are a result of:

- lack of oxygen when being born
- malaria
- diarrhoea
- illnesses after being born
- pneumonia
- being born too early.

Other reasons also have an impact on rates, including HIV/AIDs, conflict, malnutrition and lack of safe water. These mortality rates can be decreased using simple strategies such as more child vaccinations, more readily available antibiotics, bed nets, food programmes and more support for mothers.

The level of poverty a child is born into affects his/her chances of survival: children born into poverty, rather than wealth, are twice as likely to die before they reach 5 years old. If a mother has received an education, even just to primary level, her children are more likely to live past the age of 5.

VIDEO LINK

Check out the video about child mortality at www. brightredbooks.net/ N5ModernStudies.

WHAT AREAS ARE AFFECTED?

There is a significant difference in child mortality rates between developed and less-developed countries. In 2011 only 1.4% of under-5 deaths occurred in developed countries.

As less-developed countries have higher poverty rates and lower access to education it is no surprise that child mortality levels are higher in these regions, for example a child born in Ethiopia is 30 times more likely to die before he/she reaches the age of 5 than a child born in Western Europe. In 2011 child mortality rates in less-developed regions were eight times higher than those in developed regions. The region with the highest level of child mortality is sub-Saharan Africa: 82% of the total under-5 deaths occur within this region. For every 1000 live births there are 121 children who will not reach 5 years old. Southern Asia has the second highest rates, with 66 out of every 1000 born not reaching 5.

WHAT PROGRESS HAS BEEN MADE?

Although the global population has increased, the level of child mortality has decreased from 12 million in 1990 to 6.9 million in 2011, which is a decline of 42%. Child mortality within developed countries has decreased by 58% and by 42% in less-developed countries. Within less-developed countries five out of nine regions have cut their rates by more than half. Eastern Asia and northern Africa have actually reached the Millennium Development Goal target.

contd

Some areas of sub-Saharan Africa have made progress in lowering child mortality. Fourteen countries that were experiencing 40 or more deaths per 1000 live births in 1990 halved their rates by 2010. Countries such as Madagascar decreased rates by 60%.

After analysing the annual figures from 1990 to 2011 it is clear that some countries have not made enough progress to allow them to meet the fourth Millennium Development Goal by the target year of 2015. Overall only developed countries are likely to meet the target.

Although there has been global improvements, rates within sub-Saharan Africa and southern Asia are continuing to increase. There are 24 countries that experience 100 or more deaths per 1000 live births: 23 are part of sub-Saharan Africa and one is in southern Asia.

Region	Progress
Latin America and the Caribbean	Predicted to meet target
Northern Africa	Predicted to meet target
Sub-Saharan Africa	Not likely to meet target
Eastern Asia	Predicted to meet target
Caucasus and Central Asia	Not likely to meet target
Southern Asia	Not likely to meet target
Western Asia	Predicted to meet target
Oceania	Not likely to meet target

Source: UN Children's Fund.

The number of children who die before their first birthday is also closely monitored and is referred to as neonatal deaths. It has been found that while the child mortality rate is decreasing the share of deaths that occur before the child's first birthday is actually increasing: more children are dying before their first birthday than ever before. In 1990 37% of child deaths were occurring within a year of being born. By 2010 this had increased to 40%. Although eastern Asia has significantly lowered its child mortality rates, 57% of child deaths are neonatal deaths.

Case study: UNICEF and Ethiopia

In 2004 UNICEF set up a health programme which involved a team of 34,000 workers being sent to 15,000 villages to support families in Ethiopia. The aim of this programme was to help Ethiopia reduce the number of preventable child deaths. The workers provided vital health care to children, such as vaccinations, and trained local families. These trained families are known as 'model families' and have a deeper understanding of basic health care that can be carried out at home. The model families can now support and teach other people in their village.

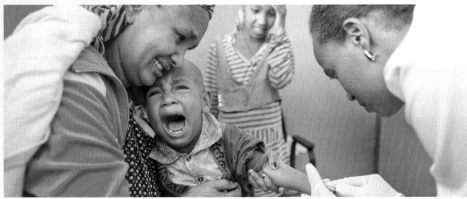

ONLINE

Check out the UNICEF Ethiopia site at www.brightredbooks.net/N5ModernStudies.

FACT

189 world leaders agreed to reach the Millennium Development Goals by 2015.

DON'T FORGET

Sub-Saharan Africa only contains 12% of the world's population therefore the size of its population is not the reason why it has higher child mortality rates.

THINGS TO DO AND THINK ABOUT

1 'Child mortality rates have decreased throughout the world. All regions have decreased child mortality at the same rate and child mortality is no longer an international concern.' UN spokesperson.

Using the information above, explain why the view of the UN spokesperson is selective in the use of facts?

2 In what ways do high child mortality rates have an impact on a country in the long term?

3 You have now studied three of the Millennium Development Goals. In what ways do hunger and level of education impact on child mortality?

ONLINE TEST

Revise your knowledge of the world issue of child mortality at www.brightredbooks.net/N5ModernStudies.

SOURCE-BASED QUESTIONS: CONCLUSIONS

It is important that you are able to understand sources and draw your own conclusions about the information. At National 5 level you are expected to be able to draw conclusions based on information from between two and four written or numerical sources. The question will be worth 8 marks.

TOP TIPS

A conclusion is an overall statement about an issue that is supported with evidence. A strong conclusion always has evidence to back it up. Would you believe a point in a debate if there were no evidence to support it?

Your answer should therefore have two parts:
1   your conclusion/overall statement
2   evidence from the sources to support your conclusion/overall statement.

You should try and link information between sources and within sources. A well-developed conclusion will have evidence from more than one source.

You will not achieve full marks unless you provide evidence from the sources to back up your conclusions.

Be careful that you don't just describe the information in the sources. This is a common mistake that candidates make. You will not receive any marks if you just copy the information from the source. To make sure that you don't do this consider the following points:
● What does the information actually show?
● What can you learn from it?

Imagine the points you are asked to make a conclusion about are actually questions. For example:

You should reach a conclusion about each of the following:
● *United Nations membership* = What changes to membership have occurred?
● *Action taken by the United Nations* = What action does the United Nations take?
● *Voluntary agencies and the United Nations* = What relationship is there between voluntary agencies and United Nations?

When practising your conclusion questions try writing the conclusion in one colour and the evidence in another. That way you can easily see if you have included both elements in your answer.

Steps:
1   Read the sources of information that you have been provided with.
2   Read the question: what are you required to make conclusions about?
3   Decide on your overall statement.
4   Decide what evidence you can use to support your point. Make sure you try and link information between sources.
5   Structure your conclusion.

Structure:

> A conclusion that can be made about _____ is _____. I think
> this because Source 1/2/3/4 states _____. Source 1/2/3/4 also
> states _____.

EXAMPLE QUESTION

SOURCE 1: Use of the death penalty

Supporters of the death penalty argue that it is an effective deterrent against crime. They state that the tougher the punishment the less likely people are to commit the crime.

The number of countries that have the death penalty as a form of punishment is dropping, but the death penalty is still being used on a global scale. In 2003, 28 countries completed executions; by 2012 this had decreased to 21.

China, Iran, North Korea, Yemen and the USA executed the most people during 2012. Evidence suggests that China has executed more people than the rest of the world put together. There is no exact figure, as the Chinese government will not share this information. Iran has the second-highest number of executions.

Not all death penalty sentences are carried out within international law, for example Yemen executed two prisoners for crimes they had carried out when they were below the death penalty age limit of 18. Belarus has carried out executions that have gone against the rights of the prisoners under Articles 6, 7 and 14 of the International Covenant on Civil and Political Rights.

In 2011, 1923 people were sentenced to death in 63 countries. This number dropped in 2012, when 1722 people in 58 countries were sentenced to death.

Overall there are almost five times as many countries not carrying out the death penalty as those who do.

SOURCE 2: Executing and non-executing countries

Year	Executing countries	Non-executing countries
1991	32	48
1995	41	59
2000	27	75
2005	22	86
2010	23	96
2012	21	97

SOURCE 3: 2012 executing countries

SOURCE 4: Case study: Belarus and the death penalty

- Belarus is the only country in Europe and Central Asia that continues to use the death penalty as a form of punishment.
- In 2012 evidence indicates that at least three men were executed, but information about death penalty cases is kept private therefore the number could be a lot higher.
- Uladzlau Kavalyou and Dzymitry Kanavalau were arrested for suspicion of being involved in bomb attacks in Belarus in 2011. They received unjust trails, which resulted in their execution.
- This case broke international law as neither of the prisoners was given the opportunity to appeal.
- Both prisoners stated that they had been forced to admit to their charges through torture and threats.
- Uladzlau Kavalyou was executed despite the UN Human Rights Committee's orders not to until they had reviewed the case.

Using Sources 1, 2, 3 and 4 above, what conclusions can be drawn about the use of the death penalty as a form of punishment?

You should reach a conclusion about each of the following.

- changes in the use of the death penalty
- the country carrying out the highest number of executions
- Belarus and its use of the death penalty.

Your conclusions must be supported by evidence from the sources. You should link information within and between sources in support of your conclusions.

Your answer must be based on all four sources.

8 marks

(Source: Amnesty International 2012)

 THINGS TO DO AND THINK ABOUT

Try out the example question above. Remember to use the two-part structure when answering. Your teacher or lecturer will be able to give you advice on your answer.

GLOSSARY

Act
A bill which has received royal assent and become a law

Additional Member System
The voting system used in the Scottish Parliament, which gives voters two votes in the hope of achieving a more proportional overall result

amendments
changes made to bills, usually by parliament

Arab Spring
A series of revolutions against governments of Arab countries

ballot paper
The piece of paper you place your vote on in an election

benefit cap
a limit on the amount of social security payments (benefits) which a person or family can receive from the UK government

benefit fraud
giving false information to the government, to get more social security payments than one is entitled to

benefit trap
when the amount of social security payments one can receive is greater than the amount one would get from working: putting one off trying to get a job

benefits
social security payments from the government

bicameral
A parliamentary system which has two houses, like the House of Commons and the House of Lords in the UK Parliament

Bill
A draft law

BRICS
Brazil, Russia, India, China and South Africa. Up and coming economic world powers.

Cabinet
The most important members of a government; a group of people who assist the Prime / First Minister and are in charge of different government departments

candidates
people who want to be elected

canvassing
going door-to-door to meet voters in an election campaign

capital expenditure
spending money on large projects like bridges and schools

coalition
a government made up of two or more different parties

collective responsibility
the rule that members of a **cabinet** must support the decision in public, even if they disagree with it

Committees
groups of MSPs or MPs (and sometimes members of the House of Lords) who meet to discuss and investigate certain policy areas

constituency
an area which elects an MP or MSP

constituency link
when it is very clear who represents an area in parliament

constituents
people who live in an area represented by an MP or MSP

council tax
a tax which adults must pay to the local council, which pays for local council services like parks and waste collection

crossbenchers
Members of the House of Lords who are not a member of any political party, and are therefore neutral

custodial sentence
being sent to prison or a young offenders' institution as punishment for a crime

debate
when MPs, MSPs or councillors discuss an issue or suggested law; an opportunity for different opinions to be heard

Decision Time
When MSPs vote on all the bills and statements of the day: held in the afternoon

Deforestation
The cutting down or removal of forest trees

democracy
a political system where people are given a say in the decisions made for the country

demonstrations
when people meet to show support for, or opposition to, something or someone

devolution
the passing of power from one part of government to a lower part of government

devolved matters
policy areas the Scottish Parliament gets to make decisions about

disproportional
too large or small in proportion to something else, like when a share of seats lower than the share of votes a party wins in an election

division
a vote in the UK Parliament

election campaigns
the time when political parties and candidates are allowed to try to win votes

electorate
the people allowed to vote in an election

entrepreneurs
people who start up and run businesses

evaluative terminology
words which clearly show the value of something; how big or small it is

favelas
a shanty town in Brazil with poorly built and overcrowded houses

federal republic
a way to run a country where there is one central government which has authority over the whole country and state governments with specific state powers

first-generation immigrants
people who have moved into a country

First Minister's Question Time
the time when MSPs get to ask the First Minister questions about the government's or the First Minister's actions

First Past The Post system
The electoral system used to elect MPs to the UK Parliament

fuel poverty
when after paying for fuel a family has less money than the official poverty line; or when a household needs to spend more than 10% of its income on fuel to maintain a reasonable heat in the home

G20
a group of 19 countries and the EU who come together to improve the world's economy

gang culture
the lifestyle of illegal behaviour which gang members live

general election
When Members of the UK Parliament are elected by the public

glass ceiling effect
the combination of factors which stops many women reaching the top of their professional careers: the top positions can be seen, but something is stopping many reaching it

government
The group of MPs or MSPs who decide how the country will run, after winning the election

House of Commons
the lower house of the UK Parliament, made up of MPs elected by the public

House of Lords
the upper house of the UK Parliament, made up of appointed peers, (elected) hereditary peers, and bishops from the Church of England

human rights
rights that everyone is entitled to

hustings
public meetings where candidates in an election speak in front of, and are asked questions by, the public

hypothesis
an educated guess about what might be found out about a research topic; it can be proven or disproven

ideologies
ideas about how a country should be run

industrial action
action taken by members of a trade union designed to disrupt production, like a strike

legislation
laws, at all stage of being passed

lobbying
putting pressure on decision-makers, usually by actually going to meet them in person

local councils
the level of government which makes decisions for their local areas

majority government
when a party wins an election with more than half of the seats in parliament

mandate
the authority to carry out a policy or policies

manifesto
a document containing plans for what a political party will do if they win the election

means-tested
benefit payments which vary depending on your circumstances (usually how much you earn)

media
TV, radio and newspapers as a way of communicating with the public

Millennium Development Goals
a list of 8 goals that were agreed by the members of the United Nations to deal with poverty, hunger, disease, illiteracy, the environment and discrimination against women

minority ethnic
belonging to any ethnic (racial) group which is not white

minority government
when a party wins more seats than any other, but less than half of the seats in parliament, but decides to form a government anyway

minutes
a record of what has been said in a meeting

motion
the topic of a debate

National Minimum Wage
the minimum pay per hour almost all workers are entitled to by law

negative campaigning
when parties or candidates in an election focus on the failings of their opponents, instead of their own strengths

non-custodial sentences
any punishment other than prison received for a crime

occupational pensions
a way of saving for retirement which is arranged by the employer

opposition
all parties other than those in government

parliament
where laws are made

party election broadcasts
TV and radio broadcasts made by political parties to persuade people to vote for them

peers
members of the House of Lords

petitions
a request, usually signed by many people, which is presented to decision-makers

plea
the opportunity the accused has in a trial to say whether they think they are 'guilty' or 'not guilty'

plurality
the single biggest number, but less than half

policy
a course of action proposed by a political party

GLOSSARY

positive action
the steps an employer can take to encourage people from groups which have previously been discriminated against to apply for jobs

poverty
being extremely poor, which can be defined in many ways

poverty line
a way of measuring poverty: 60% of the median (the middle value if all were lined up) income in the UK

Presiding Officer
the person in charge of the debating chamber in the Scottish Parliament

pressure group
a group of people who share an interest or concern, and want to influence decision-makers in favour of their interest

Prime Minister's Question Time
the time when MPs get to ask the Prime Minister questions about the government's or the Prime Minister's actions

Private Member's Bill
a bill proposed by an MP or MSP who is not a member of the government

proportional
matching in proportion to something else, like when a share of seats matches the share of votes a party wins in an election

prosecute
to carry out legal court action against someone

public sector
the organisations in the country paid for by the government through tax money

Question Time
when MPs or MSPs get to ask government ministers about their actions

quota
the amount of votes required to be elected under the Single Transferable Vote voting system

rebellion
when MPs vote against their party leadership's wishes

recession
when production and trade in a country reduces so a country becomes less wealthy

referendum
a public vote on an issue

remand
to place a defendant on bail or in custody

representative democracy
when people choose people to speak up for them when decisions are made, like MPs or MSPs

reserved matters
policy areas the UK Parliament gets to make decisions about

Royal Assent
when the monarch (King or Queen) officially approves a law; now done automatically

safe seat
a parliamentary seat where the winner is almost guaranteed

sectarianism
behaving in a bigoted or narrow-minded way to a person or people because they follow a different religion

shop steward
a trade union representative in a workplace

Single Transferable Vote
the voting system used for Scottish local council elections, which is designed to give each area 3 or 4 representatives to each area, and give proportional results

Speaker
the person in charge of the debating chamber in the UK Parliament

state pension
the money every elderly person above a certain age receives from the UK government

surgeries
open meetings held by representatives (like MPs, MSPs and councillors) where members of the public can raise concerns

surplus votes
votes which a local council election candidate has left over after already being elected – above the quota

tactical voting
when voters vote for a candidate other than their favourite, just to avoid their least-favourite candidate winning

tax avoidance
legally taking action to lower the amount of tax you have to pay

trade unions
organisations which represent groups of workers

turnout
the share of people who could have voted who did vote

unicameral
a parliamentary system which has one house, like the Scottish Parliament

United Nations
an international organisation dedicated to promoting peace, security and human rights

verdict
the final decision in a court case; usually 'guilty' or 'not guilty'

ward
a local council area, which elects 3 or 4 local councillors

wasted votes
votes for candidates who are not elected

welfare state
a system whereby the government takes responsibility of protecting the health and well-being of its citizens